225 SPECIES IN FULL COLOR

INSECTS

A GUIDE TO FAMILIAR AMERICAN INSECTS

by
HERBERT S. ZIM, Ph.D.
and
CLARENCE COTTAM, Ph.D.

Director, Welder Wildlife Foundation;
Formerly Assistant Director, U.S. Fish and Wildlife Service

ILLUSTRATED BY
JAMES GORDON IRVING

Sponsored by
The Wildlife Management Institute

A GOLDEN NATURE GUIDE

GOLDEN PRESS • NEW YORK

FOREWORD

This book is one of the most ambitious attempted in the Golden Nature Guide series. Because of its scope, unusual problems had to be solved all along the way. The end was achieved because of the cooperation of many people who felt it important to have a reliable beginner's guide to insects. The authors express their appreciation to all who participated.

The artist, James Gordon Irving, made a superb contribution. His wife, Grace Crowe Irving, helped in field studies, collecting, and research. Robert T. Mitchell was most helpful—in compiling lists from which the original selections were made; in checking data; in preparing maps. Specimens came from the Patuxent Research Refuge, the U.S. National Museum, and Melville W. Osborne, Rahway, N. J. Numerous specialists generously offered suggestions on the plates—William D. Field, Edward A. Chapin, William H. Anderson, Austin H. Clark, George B. Vogt, Reece I. Sailer, Hahn W. Capps, O. L. Cartwright, Paul W. Oman, Ashley B. Gurney, Barnard D. Burks, Karl V. Krombein, Ross H. Arnett, Jr., Marion R. Smith, Alan Stone, John G. Franclemont, Arthur B. Gahan, Curtis W. Sabrosky, Grace B. Glance, C. F. W. Muesebeck, and others.

In the present revision, six additional pages of information have been added, plus a listing of scientific names. We hope readers will find this fuller and more attractive volume more useful.

H.S.Z.

C.C.

REVISED EDITION

USING THIS BOOK

By dealing only with common, important, and showy insects, this book will help the novice begin a fascinating study. To identify an insect, turn to the key to the insect groups (orders) on pages 4 and 5. This key may place your specimen within one of 16 groups. Thumb through the section indicated to find your specimen or something similar. Study all the illustrations to become aware of insects you might not otherwise notice. You may thus become able to identify some at first sight. Don't be disappointed with failures. It may take an expert a year or more, after finding an insect, to make a final identification. If you can place in their proper orders a quarter of the insects you find, you have made a good start.

Insects in this book are often shown on their food plants. Immature forms often appear with the adult. If you cannot identify an immature insect, try to raise it to maturity.

In advanced study the Latin scientific names of species are used for greater precision in designation. Scientific names of species illustrated in this book are given on pages 155-157.

On plates, approximate lengths are given in inches ("w." indicates width of wings).

Range maps show occurrence of species within the United States, just over the Mexican border, and about 200 miles northward into Canada. Since distribution of many species is little known, ranges given are only approximate. Where ranges of two or more insects appear on one map, each has a different color or line pattern, as in the sample here. A red tint over a line pattern indicates greater abundance (as on page 17). Each caption is on or next to the color to which it refers.

GRASSHOPPERS, ROACHES, AND THEIR KIN (Orthoptera), pages 17-28. Medium to large insects. Live on land. Forewings leathery. Hindwings folded fan-like (some have no wings). Development gradual. Chewing mouth-parts.

EARWIGS (Dermaptera), page 29. Small insects with typical pincer-like tail. Usually four small wings. Segmented antennae. Development gradual.

TERMITES (Isoptera), pages 30-31. Ant-like insects, small and soft-bodied. Some have four long wings. Live in colonies. Specialized "castes" for working, fighting. Chewing mouth-parts. Development gradual.

LICE (Anoplura), page 32. Small, wingless insects with piercing and sucking mouth-parts. Body flattened. Legs with claws for clinging to warm-blooded animals.

LEAFHOPPERS, APHIDS, AND SCALE INSECTS (Homoptera), pages 33-41. Small to medium insects, most with two pairs of similar wings held sloping at sides of body. Jointed beak for sucking attached to base of head. Land insects. Some scale-like.

TRUE BUGS (Hemiptera), pages 42-49. Range from small to large in size. Two pairs of wings, with forewings partly thickened. Jointed beak for sucking arises from front of head. Development is gradual.

DRAGONFLIES AND THEIR KIN (Odonata), pages 50-51. Fairly large insects with two pairs of long, equal-sized wings. Body long and slender. Antennae short. Immature insects are aquatic. Development in three stages.

MAYFLIES (Ephemerida) **AND STONEFLIES** (Plecoptera), page 52. Both with two pairs of transparent, veined wings. In mayflies, hind wings are smaller; in stoneflies they are larger. Mayflies have long, 2- or 3-pronged tails.

NERVE-WINGED INSECTS (Neuroptera), pages 53-55. The two pairs of wings, usually equal in size, are netted with veins. Four stages of development: egg, larva, pupa, and adult. Chewing mouth-parts. Long antennae.

SCORPIONFLIES (Mecoptera), page 56. Small insects with two pairs of slender, generally spotted wings. Legs long. Antennae long also. Beak-like, chewing mouth-parts. Larvae live in soil.

CADDISFLIES (Trichoptera), page 57. Most larvae live in fresh water. Some build ornamented case. Adults with two pairs of wings with long, silky hairs and with long antennae. Mouth-parts reduced.

MOTHS AND BUTTERFLIES (Lepidoptera), pages 58-101. Medium to large insects with two pairs of scaly wings. Sucking mouth-parts. Antennae knob-like or feathery. Development in four stages.

FLIES AND THEIR KIN (Diptera), pages 102-108. Two-winged, small to medium insects, with sucking mouth-parts. Antennae small, eyes large. Second pair of wings reduced to balancing organs. Development in four stages.

BEETLES (Coleoptera), pages 109-135. Forewings modified to thickened covers. Hind wings thin, folded. Size from small to large. Chewing mouth-parts. Antennae usually short. All have four life stages. Some aquatic.

BEES, WASPS, AND ANTS (Hymenoptera), pages 136-149. Small to medium-size insects; many social or colonial. Two pairs of thin, transparent wings. Hindwings smaller. Mouth-parts for chewing or sucking. Only insects with "stingers." Development in four stages.

SEEING INSECTS

You can't help seeing insects, for they are found every-where, even in the Antarctic. They have been on this earth some 200 million years, and seem here to stay. More insects and more kinds of insects are known than all other animals visible to the naked eye. Insects have been called man's worst enemy. They are. But some have economic value, and for other reasons we would be hard put to exist without them. Insects are gems of natural beauty, zoological mysteries, and a constant source of interest.

WHAT INSECTS ARE   Insects are related to crabs and lobsters. Like these sea animals they possess a kind of skeleton on the *outside* of their bodies. The body itself is composed of three divisions: head, thorax, and abdomen. The thorax has three segments, each with a pair of jointed legs; so an insect normally has six legs. Most insects also have two pairs of wings attached to the thorax, but some have only one pair, and a few have none at all. Insects usually have two sets of jaws, two kinds of eyes—simple and compound—and one pair of antennae.

So much for the typical insects, but many common ones

PARTS OF AN INSECT

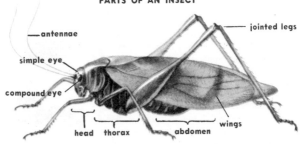

antennae

jointed legs

simple eye

compound eye

head   thorax   abdomen   wings

are not typical. The thorax and abdomen may appear to run together. Immature stages (larvae) of many insects are worm-like, though their six true legs and perhaps some extra false ones may be counted. Immature insects are often difficult to identify. It is also hard to tell the sex of some insects. In some groups males are larger or have larger antennae or different markings. The female is sometimes marked by a spear-like ovipositor for laying eggs extending from the base of the abdomen.

INSECT RELATIVES A number of insect-like animals are confused with insects. Spiders have only two body divisions and four pairs of legs. They have no antennae. Some spiders do not live in webs. Other insect-like animals have the head and thorax joined like the spiders. Crustaceans have at least five pairs of legs and two pairs of antennae. Most live in water (crab, lobster, shrimp), but the lowly sowbug is a land crustacean. Centipedes and millipedes have many segments to their bodies with one pair of legs (centipedes) or two pairs (millipedes) on each. Centipedes have a pair of long antennae; millipedes have a short pair. Millipedes often coil up when disturbed.

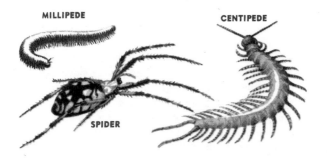

MILLIPEDE

CENTIPEDE

SPIDER

NUMBER OF INSECTS   The insect group is by far the largest group of animals in the world. Over 900,000 species have been identified, but one authority says this may be only 10 percent of the insects yet to be discovered. The class of insects is divided into some 25 orders. One order encompasses the moths and butterflies; one, the termites; another, the beetles. The beetles alone include some 250,000 species. There are more kinds of beetles than kinds of all other animals known, outside the insects. Butterflies and moths total over 110,000 kinds. Bees, wasps, and ants number 100,000; true bugs, 55,000 or more. The student of insect life need never lack material. Over 15,000 species have been found around New York City. Anyone can find a thousand species in his vicinity if he looks for small insects as well as for large, showy ones.

INSECTS AND MAN   Whether certain insects are to be considered helpful to man or otherwise, depends as much on man as it does on insects. Our ways of farming and raising animals have provided some insects which might otherwise be rare with conditions enabling them to multiply a thousandfold. Only about 1 percent of insects are harmful, but these destroy about 10 percent of our crops, causing a loss of billions of dollars annually. Other insects are parasitic on other animals, and some are known to carry diseases.

On the other hand, this would be a sorry world without insects. We would have no apples, grapes, or clover, much less cotton, and fewer oranges and garden vegetables, for these and many other common plants depend on insects to pollinate their flowers. And there would be no honey, of course. Some insects aid the process of decay, a process that is essential to life. Some insects help control others, and all help maintain a balance in nature.

INSECTS IN THEIR PLACE   In the broad view, insects play an important natural role, not only in ways that benefit man but as food for many kinds of fish, amphibians, birds, and mammals. Many of our songbirds depend almost entirely on an insect diet. Every fisherman knows how fresh-water game fish go after insects. Insects help make our rich plant life and wildlife possible. Keep this broad view in mind when people start talking about widespread insect control—something that may become possible with newer chemicals. Local control may be successful and useful to man, but control on a large scale might cause more harm than it would prevent, because insects are so important to most other kinds of life about us.

CONTROL OF INSECTS   There are ways to supplement the natural control of insects by birds and other animals. We encourage those harmless insects which prey on harmful kinds. We can exclude insects with screens, discourage them with repellents, trap them or poison them. Many of the newer poisons are highly effective. But since there are so many kinds of insects which live and feed in so many different ways, there is no single best method to get rid of them. Yet, with concerted effort some dangerous insects have been wiped out over fairly large areas. A unique example of this was the complete destruction of the Mediterranean fruit fly, which menaced the citrus crop in 20 Florida counties.

If you have an important insect problem, consult your local Board of Health or your County Agent. Often entomologists (insect specialists) at universities or museums can be of assistance. Finally, you can turn to the U. S. Department of Agriculture, Bureau of Entomology, Washington 25, D. C., where experts are working on nearly every phase of insect life and insect control.

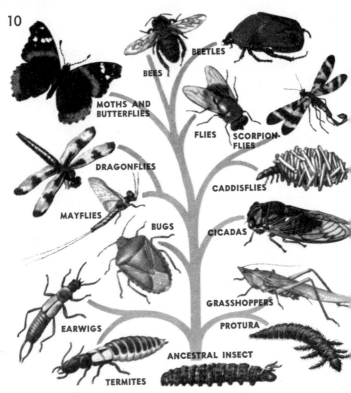

BEETLES

BEES

MOTHS AND
BUTTERFLIES

FLIES

SCORPION-
FLIES

DRAGONFLIES

CADDISFLIES

MAYFLIES

BUGS

CICADAS

GRASSHOPPERS

EARWIGS

PROTURA

ANCESTRAL INSECT

TERMITES

FAMILY TREE OF INSECTS The ancestor of all insects
was probably a segmented worm-like creature much like
primitive protura, silverfish, springtails, and kin. As long
as 200 million years ago, roaches and other insects were
common. Today there are 20 to 26 orders of insects (depending on the classification), including over 600,000
species. Most of the 12,000 kinds of fossil insects identified
are similar to living species. For relationships of insects,
see "family tree" above.

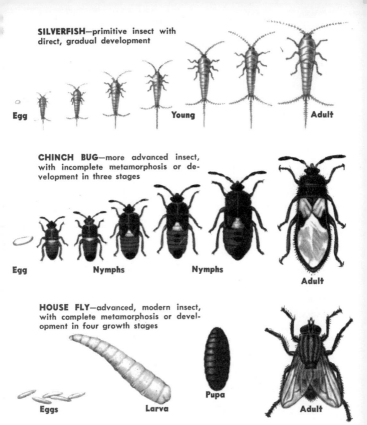

SILVERFISH—primitive insect with direct, gradual development

Egg　　　　　　　　Young　　　　　　　Adult

CHINCH BUG—more advanced insect, with incomplete metamorphosis or development in three stages

Egg　　　Nymphs　　　Nymphs　　　Adult

HOUSE FLY—advanced, modern insect, with complete metamorphosis or development in four growth stages

Eggs　　Larva　　Pupa　　Adult

Insects follow different developmental patterns. In the simplest, the newly hatched insect is like a miniature adult. It grows and molts (sheds its skin) till it reaches adult size. In incomplete metamorphosis an immature nymph hatches, grows, develops wings, and by stages becomes an adult. Complete metamorphosis involves (1) egg, (2) larva, (3) pupa or resting stage, (4) adult.

INTERIOR OF A GRASSHOPPER (Side View)

Heart

Blood vessel

Brain

Mouth

Anus

Digestive tract (red)   Ganglion

Gastric caeca

Nerve cord

INSECT STRUCTURE is marked by three body divisions (page 6), six jointed legs, one pair of antennae, and usually one or two pairs of wings. The outer covering, or exoskeleton, is often horny. Mouth-parts are complicated. Internally, insects possess many of the organs which are further developed in higher animals. They have a digestive tract and auxiliary digestive organs. Breathing is done by air tubes spreading internally from openings called spiracles. The head is tube-like; blood circulation is simple. Respiration, digestion, and circulation are shown in the longitudinal section (above) and cross-section (left) of the grasshopper, a typical insect.

Digestive tract

Blood vessel

Spiracle

Nerves

Air tubes

CROSS-SECTION

The nervous system (below) shows the simple brain, which exerts very little control over the body. Ganglions serve as nerve centers for nearby parts of the body.

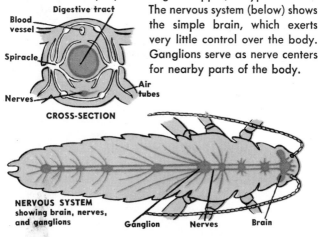

NERVOUS SYSTEM
showing brain, nerves,
and ganglions

Ganglion   Nerves   Brain

FLY—mouth for lapping

BUTTERFLY—mouth for sucking nectar

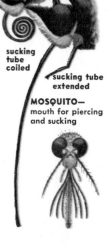

sucking tube coiled

sucking tube extended

MOSQUITO—mouth for piercing and sucking

ADAPTATIONS FOR FEEDING

Insect structures show vast variation. Adapted to many environments, insects live successfully in nearly every part of the world. They have digestive systems for all kinds of plant and animal food. They thrive on everything from wood to blood. A few species do not eat at all in the adult stage. Mouthparts are adapted for chewing, sucking, piercing and sucking, and lapping. Equally interesting adaptations are seen in insect wings, body coverings, and reproductive organs. The typical insect leg (as of a grasshopper) has five parts. Grasshopper hind legs are specialized for jumping. The house fly has pads which enable it to walk up windows. In honeybees, the hind leg is adapted to store and carry pollen, and the foreleg to groom and clean antennae and body. Insect structures make a fascinating study.

GRASSHOPPER—mouth for biting and chewing

compound eye

simple eye

ADAPTATIONS OF FEET

GRASSHOPPER—leg for jumping

DIVING BEETLE—leg for swimming

BUMBLEBEE—leg for carrying pollen

pollen basket

STUDYING
AND COLLECTING INSECTS

Our knowledge of many insects is still so incomplete that a serious amateur can look forward to becoming a specialist doing his own scientific research.

WHERE TO LOOK Practically everywhere: in fields, gardens, woods, roadsides, beaches and swamps; under stones, rotted logs and leaves. Look in flowers, on grass; on animals, too. You'll find insects in the air; in and on water; on and in the ground.

WHEN TO LOOK Insects are most common in late summer and early fall, but experienced collectors can find them in all seasons. Some groups of insects are more common at night; remember that when collecting. In winter, concentrate on protected spots, as under stones and bark. Watch for insects in egg cases or in the resting stage (pupae).

WHAT TO DO Studying insects is not confined to catching them and mounting them in collections. Raising live insects to study their habits is exciting. Anyone can have an insect zoo in old glass jars. Collect immature insects (larvae), provide them with proper food, and watch them grow.

Watch caterpillars shed their skins, spin a cocoon or chrysalis, and finally emerge as a moth or a butterfly. See worm-like larvae become flies or beetles. Raise a colony of ants, bees, or termites. You will learn more from live insects than from dead specimens.

Whatever you do with insects, you will need some understanding of what insects are and how they live. Use this book, then read some of the other books suggested. Most important, go out and look at insects. Catch them if you wish, but watch them first. See how they move, how they feed and what they do.

COLLECTING INSECTS An insect collection can be valuable for study or reference— if it is used. Using a collection means more than making a collection, though this step must come first. Fortunately, beginners can collect insects with simple, low-cost equipment. Not all insects are chased with a net. Hang an old bedsheet out at night with a small light in front of it. Roll the bottom into a funnel, with a jar set beneath. Insects hitting the sheet will roll down into the jar. Similar traps are described in reference books. Try the easiest methods and places first—as your window screens or near a large neon sign. Just gather the insect harvest there.

EQUIPMENT Any large, wide-mouthed jar will serve for confining and raising insects. Tie some gauze or netting over the top. To kill specimens use a wide-mouthed bottle with absorbent cotton or sawdust on the bottom, wet with a tablespoon or so of carbon tetrachloride or carbona. Cover this with a sheet of tight-fitting cardboard punched full of pinholes. Because cyanide is such a dangerous poison, cyanide bottles should be made and used only by experienced collectors. A light net with a long handle is good for catching insects on the wing. A heavier net is better for "sweeping" through the grass or for catching water insects.

Cigar boxes with a layer of heavy corrugated cardboard on the bottom to hold pins are fine for storing specimens. Use a mothball to deter insect pests. Purchase and use insect pins; ordinary ones are too heavy. Learn the tricks that make mounting neat and attractive. A book for records is essential; so are labels. Later you may want spreading boards, pinning blocks, and other accessories. Collecting and preserving specimens requires real skill. Read first; then practice with any insects you may find in your own yard. Skill will come with experience.

FIELD AND LIFE-HISTORY STUDIES may prove more interesting and exciting than collecting. Instead of learning a little about many insects, learn a lot about a few. Field studies can involve unusual problems on which there is little or no scientific information. How do ants recognize one another? How does temperature affect the flight of butterflies? How much does a caterpillar eat? Can beetles recognize color? Such problems can be investigated in your own yard if you are interested. Many insects are known only in the adult form; few facts are known about the rest of their life cycles. Constant observation of wild specimens, or detailed study of captive ones reared under natural conditions, may yield many new and interesting facts.

WALKINGSTICK
3.0"

black locust

WALKINGSTICKS are large, usually wingless insects with legs all about the same length, distinguishing them from the mantises (pp. 24-25). Walkingsticks live and feed on leaves of oak, locust, cherry, and walnut, occasionally causing damage. The female's 100 or so eggs are dropped singly to the ground to hatch the following spring. As young grow, they molt or shed their skin five or six times; otherwise they are similar to adults. Males are smaller than females.

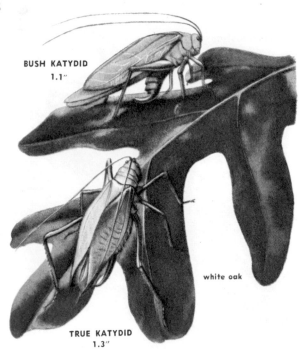

BUSH KATYDID
1.1"

white oak

TRUE KATYDID
1.3"

KATYDIDS The male of the true katydid makes the persistent "katydid" call, which, coming as often as once a second, is an accepted part of a summer's evening. Some katydids are tree dwellers, feeding on leaves of cherry, oak, maple, and apple. Others live in the grass. Most are green, with thin, leaf-like wing-covers, and so have the advantage of protective coloration. However, some species are brown or even pink. All have long antennae. At the base of the outer wings or wing-covers of the males

**ANGULAR-
WINGED
KATYDID
1.1"**

eggs

are rasps and ridges which, when rubbed like a fiddle and bow, produce the calls of the different species. Katydids hear by "ears" on the upper part of their front legs.

The females, recognized by the long ovipositor, lay their oval eggs on leaves or twigs early in the fall. About 100 to 150 are laid. When the young emerge in the spring, they resemble their parents, but are much smaller, lighter in color, and lack wings. In the South, two broods are produced each season.

MOLE
CRICKET
1.3"

CAMEL CRICKET 0.8"

MOLE AND CAMEL CRICKETS These nocturnal crickets live under rocks in moist places, or mostly underground. The large mole cricket burrows near the surface, eating young roots and killing seedlings. In the South, it destroys peanuts, strawberries, and other garden crops. The pale brown, spotted, wingless camel (or cave) cricket is identified by its high, arched back. Though a scavenger, it often becomes a nuisance around greenhouses.

Mole Cricket

MORMON CRICKET
female 1.5"   male smaller

wheat

MORMON CRICKET This serious pest of Western grains and other crops is partly controlled by insect parasites, small mammals, and birds. Gulls saved the crops of the early Mormon settlers from hordes of these crickets which descended upon them. The large, clumsy insects devour everything in their path, including each other. Some Western Indians considered them a delicacy and ate them roasted. Small clusters of eggs are laid in the ground by the female.

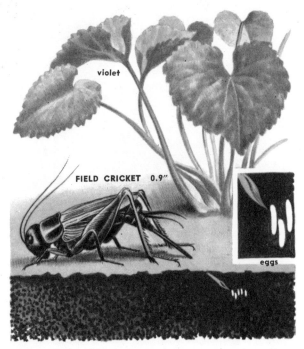

violet

FIELD CRICKET 0.9"

eggs

FIELD CRICKETS These common, large-headed, black or brown crickets are nocturnal. Their shrill musical night song is made by rubbing the forewings. Though vegetarians, they may eat other insects and each other. In captivity, these crickets make fine pets. Field crickets damage crops and occasionally invade homes, even eating clothing. Eggs are laid in the ground in fall. The young nymphs emerge in the spring and develop their adult wings in several stages.

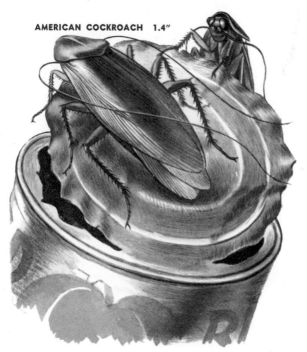

AMERICAN COCKROACH 1.4"

AMERICAN COCKROACH The common roach, bane
of housewives, traces its ancestry back to the Coal Age.
The large brown species are more common in the South.
Some kinds live in houses and barns, others in fields. They
eat all kinds of food and destroy books, rugs, and clothing. They prefer moist, dark places and usually come out
at night. This roach differs from the
smaller German roach or croton bug
(pp. 152-153). The American roach
is probably native in our tropics.

CAROLINA
MANTIS
2.3"

egg cases

MANTISES These large, slender, odd insects, the most familiar of which is generally called the praying mantis, are becoming more common. The Chinese and European mantises, introduced here more than 50 years ago, have spread widely through the East. Mantises are predators, feeding mainly on insect pests. If confined, mantises are likely to turn cannibal. They are colored a protective green and brown. Hard to see on foliage, they wait in ambush, grasping passing insects with their spiny forelegs. The wings are nearly transparent.

PRAYING MANTIS 3.5"

egg case

Lutz says these are the only insects that can look over their shoulders. In fall, after mating, the female may eat the male. She lays several hundred eggs in a frothy mass that dries like hardened brown foam. Egg cases can be found in winter and brought indoors to hatch. The young, similar to adults but light yellow, are difficult to raise. The Carolina mantis is smaller than the others. It is one of 20 native species found most commonly in the South.

Carolina

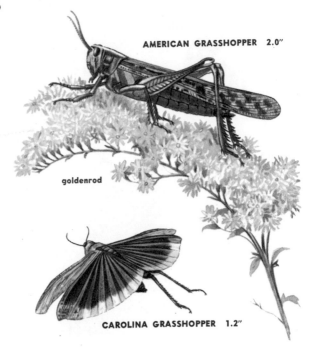

AMERICAN GRASSHOPPER 2.0"

goldenrod

CAROLINA GRASSHOPPER 1.2"

GRASSHOPPERS AND LOCUSTS are a group of closely related insects. Some species migrate; others do not. All are similar, with short antennae and large hearing organs on the abdomen. Most are good fliers, though some kinds are wingless. Locusts and grasshoppers destroy crops, especially in the West, where they are more common; but they serve as food for larger birds, small mammals, and other animals. Females lay 20 to 100 eggs in the ground or in rotted wood. See p. 28 for the life history of one species. The nymphs mature in 2 to 3 months.

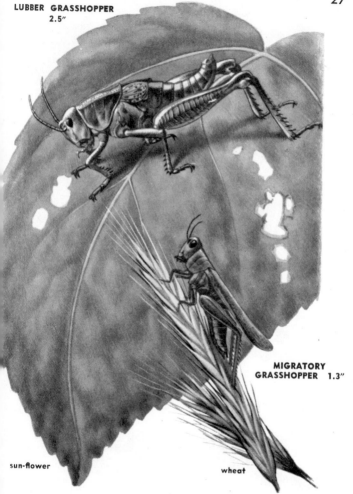

LUBBER GRASSHOPPER
2.5"

MIGRATORY
GRASSHOPPER 1.3"

sun-flower   wheat

28

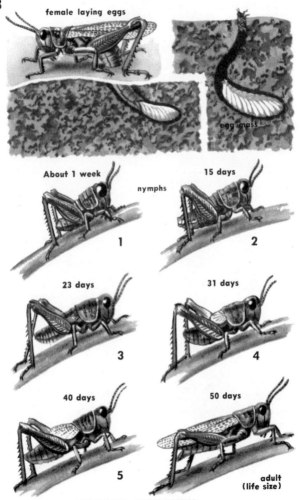

female laying eggs

egg mass

About 1 week

15 days

nymphs

1

2

23 days

31 days

3

4

40 days

50 days

5

adult
(life size)

RED-LEGGED GRASSHOPPER

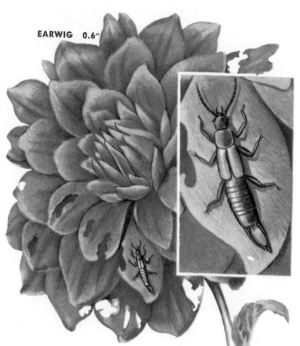

EARWIG 0.6"

EARWIGS are marked by short, leathery forewings and a pincer-like abdominal appendage which is more pronounced in males. From their abdominal glands earwigs exude a liquid with a tar-like odor. They are nocturnal, spending the day in crevices or damp places. The legend of their creeping into ears of sleeping persons is untrue. Some kinds are carnivorous, feeding on other insects. Young nymphs are wingless and gradually develop adult form.

TERMITES Though sometimes called white ants, termites are not ants, and some are not white. Of some 2,000 species, only about 40 are found in this country. Many more are tropical. These highly socialized insects live in colonies composed of four distinct castes. The king and the queen, and the winged termites which can become kings and queens of new colonies, form the first caste. The enlarged and almost helpless queen produces thousands upon thousands of eggs. Most of these hatch into whitish, blind workers who make up the second caste.

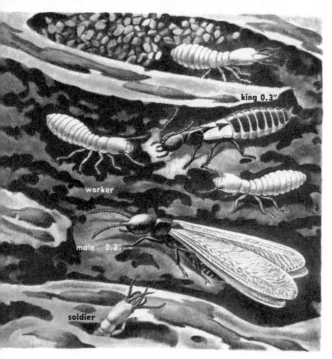

Soldiers with large heads and jaws, and nymphs which take over the task of reproduction should the king or queen die, make up the last two castes.

With the aid of protozoa living in their digestive tracts termites feed on wood and do some $40,000,000 worth of damage annually to buildings in this country. The young pass through six stages in two years as they develop into adults. Tropical termites build huge nests or mounds, often higher than a man.

HEAD LOUSE 0.1"

egg

SHORT-NOSED
CATTLE LOUSE 0.1+"   CRAB LOUSE 0.1—"   BODY LOUSE 0.1+"

LICE are minute, wingless, disease-carrying insects that live and breed on their hosts. All are parasites. Biting lice (bird lice), a distinct group, feed on hair, feathers, and fragments of skin. The sucking lice take the host's blood directly, by means of sucking mouth-parts. The hog lice (¼ in.) are the largest of this group. The head louse infects humans and is known to carry typhus, trench, and relapsing fever. Six to 12 generations of lice may mature annually. Young, similar to adults, develop rapidly.

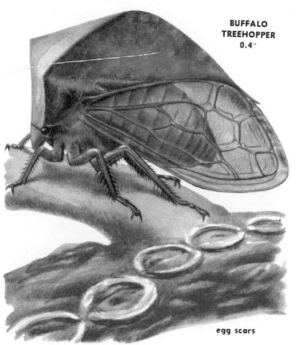

**BUFFALO
TREEHOPPER
0.4"**

egg scars

TREEHOPPERS The common green and brown treehoppers are small, winged, sucking insects of curious and
peculiar shapes. They live on many plants, feeding on the
sap. Because of their protective color and form, they are
usually noticed only when moving. Nearly 200 species
are known in this country, many with
bizarre shapes. Eggs are laid in stems
and buds, sometimes causing minor
damage. Eggs hatch the following
spring. Young are similar to adults.

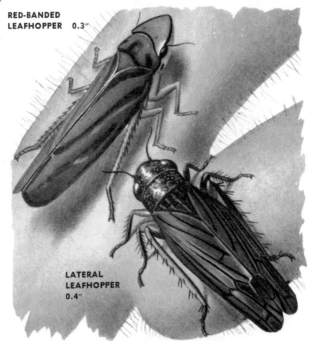

RED-BANDED
LEAFHOPPER 0.3"

LATERAL
LEAFHOPPER
0.4"

LEAFHOPPERS These attractive, slender, multicolored insects are often abundant on plants where they can feed by sucking the sap. This causes wilting and injury to grape, apple, clover, beet, and other plants. Besides, leafhoppers carry virus diseases from plant to plant and thus become serious pests.

Leafhoppers exude "honeydew" as they feed. This is a somewhat sweet surplus sap which attracts ants and bees, which feed on it. Leafhoppers are well known as prodigious jumpers. They are sometimes called dodgers

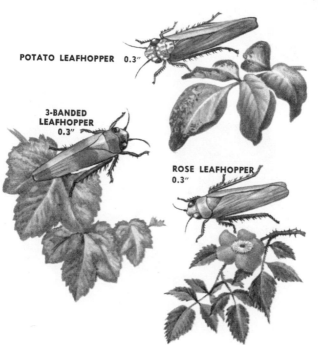

POTATO LEAFHOPPER 0.3"

3-BANDED LEAFHOPPER 0.3"

ROSE LEAFHOPPER 0.3"

because of the way they slip out of sight when disturbed.

The female lays eggs in stems and leaves. Two or more generations are produced each year. Late eggs winter over and hatch in spring. Adults hibernate and emerge in spring also. The young that hatch resemble the adults and pass through 4 or 5 nymph stages before they mature. Leafhopper populations in fields may reach as high as a million per acre. Of some 2,000 known species, about 700 are found in the United States.

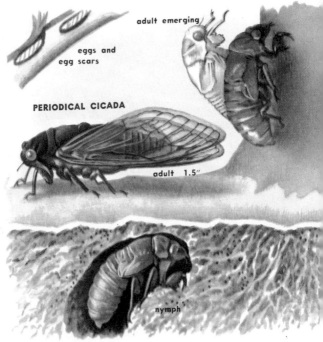

eggs and
egg scars

adult emerging

PERIODICAL CICADA

adult 1.5"

nymph

CICADAS The cicadas, whose steady hum fills the late summer air, are more often heard than seen. Males make the sharp sound with plate-like organs on the thorax. Some species are called harvestflies because of their late summer appearance; others are called 17-year locusts, though the 75 species of cicadas differ widely in the time they take to mature. The females cut slits in young twigs and deposit eggs in them. This habit causes damage in nurseries and orchards, because the slit twigs break easily in the wind. As the wingless, scaly young hatch, they drop

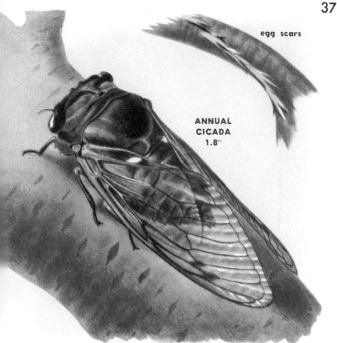

egg scars

ANNUAL CICADA
1.8"

to the ground, burrow in, and stay there 4 to 20 years (depending on the species and the latitude) as nymphs living on juices sucked from roots. The full-grown nymph climbs a tree trunk. The skin splits down the back; the adult emerges. "Broods" or large colonies may emerge en masse. Adults ordinarily live about a week—long enough to mate and start another brood. Many are eaten by birds, which gather to feast on these abundant insects.

Periodical
13-year
Annual

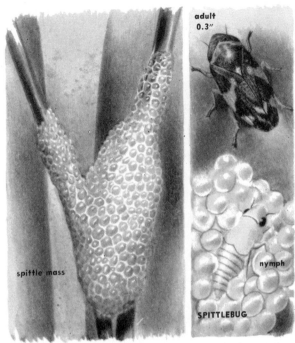

adult
0.3"

nymph

SPITTLEBUG

spittle mass

SPITTLEBUG   Female spittlebugs make a froth on stems and grasses to cover their eggs. The young nymphs make a froth also to cover themselves while feeding. Open the small mass of bubbles and you are likely to see the small, dull, squat insect inside. Spittlebugs are also called froghoppers because the adults hop about from plant to plant and seldom fly. Though spittlebugs are of minor importance, some kinds injure pine trees and various garden plants.

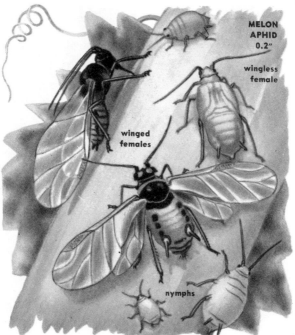

APHIDS are minute sucking insects, wingless or with transparent or colored wings. They are abundant on many plants, causing damage by sucking juices or transmitting virus diseases as they feed. Some form and live in galls. Most have complicated life histories. Only wingless females emerge from the eggs in spring. These produce generations of females all summer—sometimes a dozen. Winged females develop in the fall. Their young are normal males and females, which, after mating, produce the eggs from which new aphids emerge in spring.

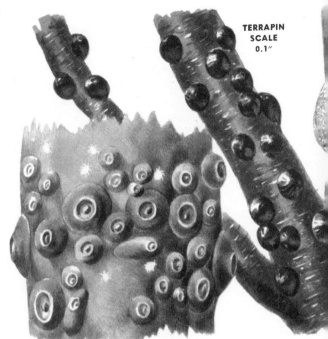

TERRAPIN
SCALE
0.1"

SAN JOSE SCALE 0.1"

SCALE INSECTS are a large group of small sucking insects. Individually minute, these insects live in colonies which often cover branches, twigs, and leaves of the plants on which they feed by sucking juices. Species differ markedly in appearance. Many have a scale-like covering and are immobile when mature. Other species lack scales, but are covered with a "honeydew" secretion eaten by bees and ants. These species move very little. Legs are poorly developed. Males are smaller and differ from the females; when mature they have small wings.

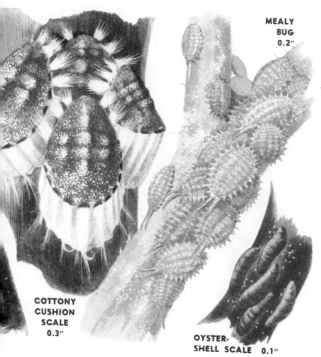

MEALY BUG 0.2"

COTTONY CUSHION SCALE 0.3"

OYSTER-SHELL SCALE 0.1"

Scale insects attack and injure citrus, apple, and other fruit trees, and greenhouse and ornamental plants. Scales are difficult to control. Ladybugs, certain small wasps, and other natural enemies are used in fighting them.

Reproduction is complicated. Most scale insects spend the winter as eggs, which the female deposits under her shell before she dies. The eggs hatch in spring and the young move to fresh growth before they settle down under a scale. Some species produce several generations of females before normal sexual reproduction takes place.

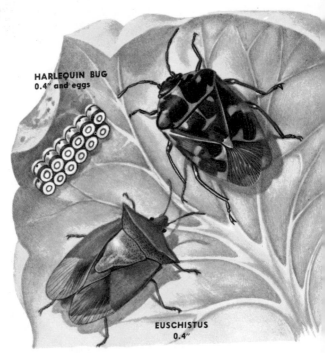

HARLEQUIN BUG
0.4" and eggs

EUSCHISTUS
0.4"

STINKBUGS AND SHIELDBUGS There are several hundred species of stinkbugs and shieldbugs in this country. All have the flattened, shield-shaped body. Most suck plant juices but some feed on other insects. Most are colored green or brown, to match their environment, and are not easily noticed. A black species common on blackberries and raspberries is so well concealed it is sometimes eaten. The colorful harlequin bug is an exception, even to its unusual eggs. The young, hatching from the eggs, pass through a series of growth stages till the nymphs

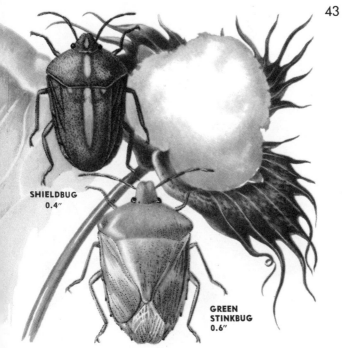

SHIELDBUG
0.4"

GREEN
STINKBUG
0.6"

become adults. The odor, which comes from two glands
on the thorax and which gives stinkbugs their name, is
also characteristic of a number of other bugs. Birds are
not bothered by the odor and commonly feed on the insects. The harlequin bug and several other species are destructive to garden crops. The shieldbugs are very similar to
stinkbugs. In these species, the shield,
which develops from the thorax, is
so large that it covers a good part of
the abdomen.

Stinkbugs
and Shieldbugs

Harlequin Bug
more common

SQUASHBUG 0.6"

TACHINID FLY 0.4"

SQUASHBUGS cause considerable damage to squash, pumpkins, gourds, and related crops by sucking juices from leaves and stems of young plants. The bugs have a strong, offensive odor. Eggs, laid in late spring, hatch in about 2 weeks. The attractive nymph is green, soon turning brown or gray. Adults hibernate over the winter. The tachinid fly, which lays its eggs in nymphs and adult squashbugs, parasitizes these pests and helps reduce their numbers.

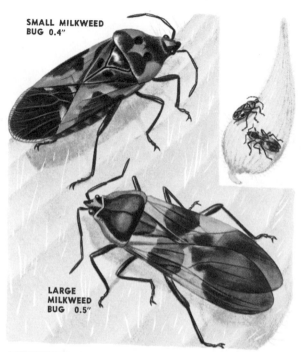

SMALL MILKWEED
BUG 0.4"

LARGE
MILKWEED
BUG 0.5"

MILKWEED BUGS These black and red or orange bugs are similar and closely related to the tiny destructive chinch bug (p. 47). About 200 species are grouped in the same family with the milkweed bugs, but most are much smaller and less attractive in color and pattern. Milkweed bugs feed on all varieties of milkweed and are of no economic importance. Adults which hibernate over the winter produce young in late spring. The nymphs mature and breed by late summer.

Small

Large

AMBUSH BUG 0.4"
feeding on aphid

AMBUSH BUG These small, oddly shaped predators form a minor group of some 25 species. Their habit is to lie concealed in flowers, grasping any small insects which may come by. Their front legs are modified for holding their victims; the mouth, for tearing and sucking. Interesting because of their bizarre forms and feeding habits, the ambush bugs lack economic importance. Not common enough to control injurious insects, they do eat beneficial ones also.

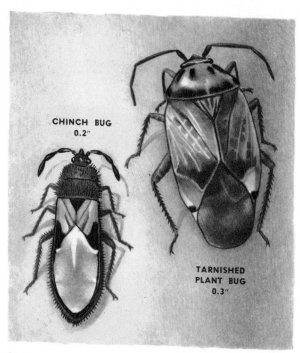

CHINCH BUG
0.2"

TARNISHED
PLANT BUG
0.3"

CHINCH BUG Though small, almost minute, chinch bugs reproduce so rapidly they overrun grain fields, destroying the crops as they feed on plant juices. The annual damage in this country runs into millions. About 500 eggs are deposited in grass or grain. Nymphs are red, becoming gray or brown with age. Two or three generations may develop in one season. The tarnished plant bug, somewhat larger, and of a related family, is destructive to many kinds of fruits.

Chinch Bug

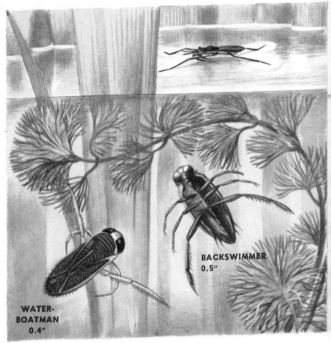

WATER-
BOATMAN
0.4"

BACKSWIMMER
0.5"

AQUATIC BUGS are found in nearly every pond and stream. A few species are marine also. All are remarkable for their adaptations to life on or below the surface. Nearly all are predaceous, attacking other insects, snails, small fish, etc. In turn, these insects are food for larger fish and water birds. The water striders, taking advantage of surface tension on water, stay on the surface without breaking through. They skate along with remarkable speed. Other water bugs spend most of their time under water. Some carry down air on the surface of their bodies

WATER STRIDERS 0.4"

GIANT WATER
BUG 2.2"

and use this for respiration. Other species breathe air that is dissolved in the water. In most cases, the young resemble the adults and mature after a series of nymphal stages. The water-boatmen have an erratic swimming pattern. The backswimmers, as their name indicates, swim on their backs, but can also fly. The giant water bugs, sometimes 2 inches or more in length, prefer quiet water. Since their bite can produce a painful swelling, the amateur collector should exercise caution. When abundant these giant water bugs are harmful in fish hatcheries.

GREEN DARNER
2.6"

nymph

DRAGONFLIES AND DAMSELFLIES These are seen near ponds and moist meadows. The former, also known as darning needles or stingers, are reputed to be dangerous. They are, but only to small insects which they eat on the wing. Dragonflies, larger than damselflies, rest with wings outstretched. The smaller, more delicate damselfly rests with wings folded. Both lay eggs on water plants or in water, and the nymphs develop there. These leave the water after several growing stages; the skin splits and the adult emerges.

TEN-SPOT DRAGONFLY 2.0"

cast skin

arrowhead

BLACKWING DAMSELFLY 1.3"

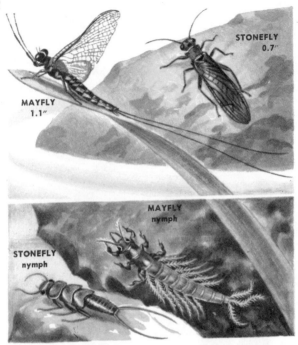

MAYFLY
1.1"

STONEFLY
0.7"

MAYFLY
nymph

STONEFLY
nymph

MAYFLIES AND STONEFLIES are unrelated (p. 4) yet are similarly adapted to aquatic environments. The 100 or so species of mayflies have transparent, veined wings and a long, forked tail. Myriads of short-lived adults are seen on mating flights or near lights. The stoneflies include some 200 species. The nymphs, like those of mayflies, live in water and are important food of fresh-water fish. Both nymphs take several years to reach the adult stage. Adult stoneflies have transparent wings, but do not fly very much or very often.

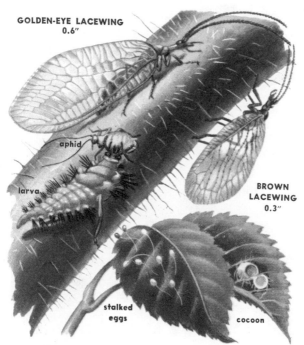

GOLDEN-EYE LACEWING
0.6"

aphid

larva

BROWN LACEWING
0.3"

stalked eggs

cocoon

LACEWINGS serve a double natural function. The adults are sometimes eaten by birds. The larvae feed on aphids and other destructive insects, earning the name aphid-lions. Many of the larvae of the 20 or more kinds of brown lacewings cover themselves with remains of aphids and other debris. Golden-eye lacewings (some 50 species) lay stalked eggs which the larvae sometimes eat. Larvae spin silky cocoons from which they emerge as delicate, thin-winged adults.

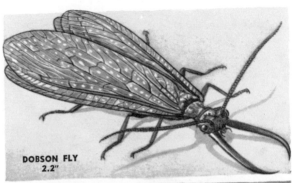

DOBSON FLY
2.2"

larva

DOBSON FLY The ferocious-looking adult male is harmless. The long mandibles are used in the mating, which ends its short life. The female lacks these exaggerated mouth-parts. She lays a mass of thousands of eggs on plants overhanging a pond or stream. The larvae emerge, drop into the water, and spend the next three years feeding on smaller water life. Fishermen prize the large larvae, called hellgrammites, as live bait.

ANT LION 1.1"

larva 0.7"

ANT LIONS are so named because the larvae of members of this family have odd feeding habits. Eggs are laid on the ground. When one hatches, the larva digs a pit in sand or sandy soil and lives almost completely buried at the bottom. Should an ant or other small insect tumble in, it is seized in powerful jaws and sucked dry. As the larva matures, it builds a silken cocoon, in which it pupates. The adult resembles a miniature, drab damselfly with short antennae.

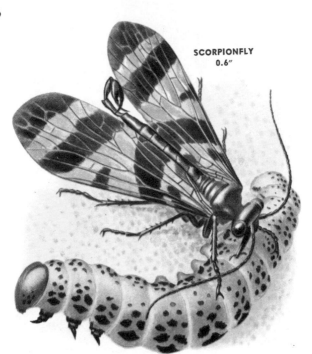

SCORPIONFLY
0.6"

SCORPIONFLIES are not poisonous, and resemble scorpions only in the modified tips of their abdomens. Eggs are deposited in the soil, where they develop into larvae. After the larvae pupate, the fly-like adults emerge to live as scavengers, feeding on dead or disabled insects. Adults are found on plants. They do not fly well or often. One group of small, almost wingless scorpionflies live in northern woods and are active even on snow in winter.

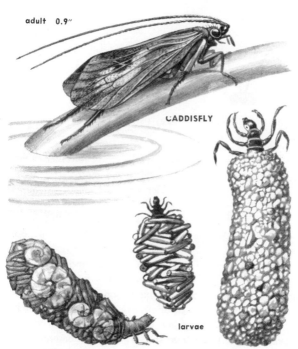

adult 0.9"

CADDISFLY

larvae

CADDISFLIES include 17 families and over 200 species. The unusual larvae, so common in fresh water, are best known. These build cases of sand or plant debris, cemented together by silk. Cases built by different species are distinctive. After the adults mate in flights over the water, the female lays several hundred eggs on submerged rocks or plants. Larvae feed on small water plants and animals, and in turn are food of many fish. Larvae pupate in the larval case.

antennae of butterfly (left) and moth

BUTTERFLIES AND MOTHS The largest, most attractive, and best-known insects are grouped together in the order Lepidoptera, the butterflies and moths. The order

scales of butterflies

includes 75 families of moths and 5 of butterflies. About 7,000 species are known in North America. All, except very few, have two pairs of wings. These and the body are covered with scales or modified hairs, which give moths and butterflies their color. The mouth-parts of adults are modified into a sucking tube which is rolled into a tight coil when not in use.

Lepidoptera have four stages of development: egg, larva (caterpillar), pupa (cocoon or chrysalis), and adult. Most butterfly eggs are laid singly or a few at a time and are unprotected. Many moths lay a large number of eggs in one place and may cover the egg mass with a protective coating which includes hairs and scales from the female's body. There is no rule of thumb for distinguishing caterpillars of

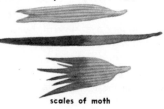

scales of moth

GIANT SWALLOWTAIL
caterpillar

moths from those of butterflies. Both have chewing mouth-parts and some kinds do tremendous damage to crops. Most caterpillars have 6 true legs on the thorax, and from 4 to 10 unjointed false legs on the abdomen. A few have irritating hairs or spines. Many caterpillars spin a silken cocoon, some-times covered with hairs, in which they pupate. The butterfly larvae make no co-coon but form a less protected chrysalis. Some Lepidoptera winter as pupae; some emerge in a short time.

pupa

cocoon

The adult moth and butterfly are usually quite different, though one group, the skippers, shows intermediate char-acteristics. Butterflies usually fly by day; moths ordinarily fly by night. The former customarily rest with their wings folded back; moths rest with their wings in a horizontal position. The antennae of butterflies are thin, ending in a knob. Those of moths never end in knobs and are often feathery. Though some butterflies are more attractive, the moths form a larger, more diverse, and more im-portant group.

MONARCH 1.3" w. 4.0"

larva on milkweed

chrysalis

MONARCH This common, attractive butterfly has spread into Asia and Australia. Males are identified by a black spot on the third vein of the hindwing. Two or three generations grow in one summer. In fall, swarms of adults migrate southward, covering entire trees when they stop to rest. They do not hibernate, as is sometimes believed. The pale green, conical eggs hatch in 3 to 5 days into larvae which feed on milkweed. The larvae are not often eaten by birds.

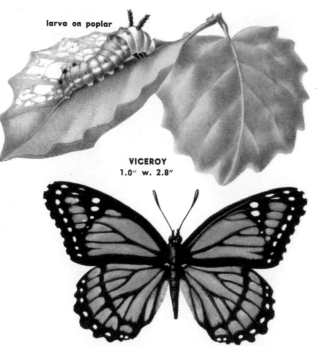

larva on poplar

VICEROY
1.0" w. 2.8"

VICEROY This butterfly is noted because in color, pattern, flight, and habits it mimics the monarch. Like the monarch it is abundant in late summer. But the viceroy is smaller and has curved black lines crossing the veins of the hindwings. Its eggs, and the larvae which feed on poplar and willow, resemble those of the purples (p. 62), to which the viceroy is related. The larvae hibernate in rolled leaves for the winter. There are two generations or more a year.

BANDED PURPLE 1.0" w. 2.9"

RED-SPOTTED PURPLE 1.0" w. 3.1"

PURPLES The banded purple has a conspicuous white band across its wings with a border of red and blue spots on the hindwings. Eggs are laid on leaves of willow, birch, and poplar, on which the larvae feed. The red-spotted purple is so named for its red spots on the under side along the wing borders and at the base of the hindwings. The larvae feed on wild cherry, willow, and other trees, preferring shaded woods.

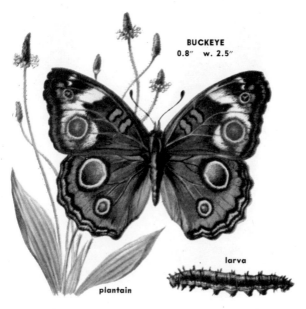

BUCKEYE
0.8" w. 2.5"

larva

plantain

BUCKEYE Though it is most common in the South and West, the buckeye is occasionally found in the North. The eye-spots make identification of the butterfly easy. The buckeye lays its green, ribbed eggs on plantain, stonecrops, or gerardia, and it is on these plants that its larvae feed. The larva forms a brown chrysalis from which the adult eventually emerges. Buckeyes are medium-sized butterflies. They are often found in open fields. In the South there are two similar species, with smaller eye-spots on the hindwings.

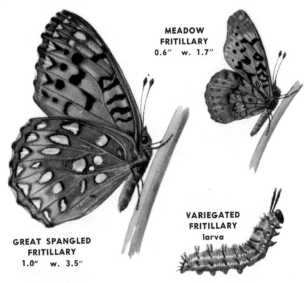

**MEADOW
FRITILLARY**
0.6" w. 1.7"

**VARIEGATED
FRITILLARY**
larva

**GREAT SPANGLED
FRITILLARY**
1.0" w. 3.5"

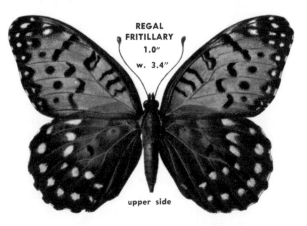

**REGAL
FRITILLARY**
1.0"
w. 3.4"

upper side

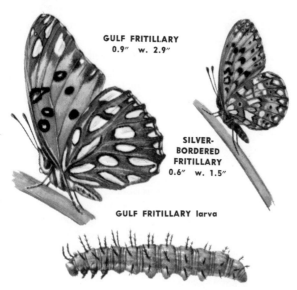

GULF FRITILLARY
0.9" w. 2.9"

**SILVER-
BORDERED
FRITILLARY**
0.6" w. 1.5"

GULF FRITILLARY larva

**REGAL
FRITILLARY**

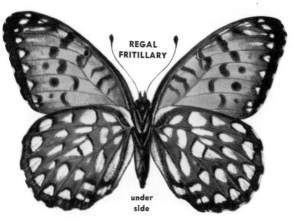

under
side

FRITILLARIES   The fritillaries, one of the largest groups of butterflies, are found not only in this country but in many other parts of the world as well. The family of which they are the most important members has front legs which are reduced in size and held close to the body. Only 4 of the 6 legs are used in walking. Fritillaries are mostly medium-sized butterflies, orange or reddish above, with silvery or light spots on the under side of the hindwings. Sometimes the males are a brighter red on top than the females.

The different species of fritillaries are distinct enough to make general statements about them difficult. The eggs are generally conical in shape and ornamented with ridges. All the caterpillars are spiny, with the spines on the head a bit longer than the others. Most feed at night on such plants as violets, goldenrods, and other composites. While the early stages of the common fritillaries are known, there are many less common species, and information on the egg and caterpillar of these species is incomplete. The chrysalis of fritillaries is usually angular, forked at the top, and bordered with knobs. It is often brownish.

Of the many fritillaries, those illustrated are among the most common and best known. The Gulf fritillary belongs to a different group from the others and is not considered a "true" fritillary.

GREAT SPANGLED FRITILLARY larva

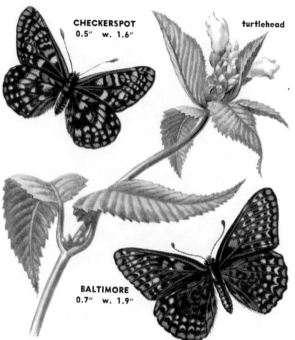

CHECKERSPOT
0.5" w. 1.6"

turtlehead

BALTIMORE
0.7" w. 1.9"

CHECKERSPOTS AND BALTIMORES Of this group of small, attractive butterflies, the two illustrated are well known. The Baltimore caterpillar is black, with orange bands and black bristles. It feeds on turtlehead and related plants. Baltimores are common locally, often in moist areas. The checkerspot lacks the brilliant orange of the Baltimore. The caterpillar is entirely black, with longer bristles. It feeds on painted cups and monkey flowers, which are common in the West.

Baltimore

Checkerspot

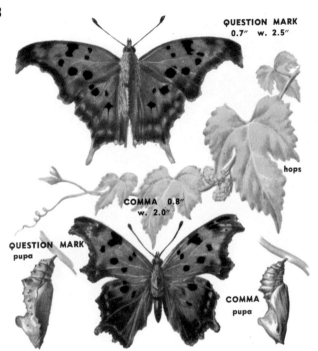

QUESTION MARK
0.7" w. 2.5"

hops

COMMA 0.8"
w. 2.0"

QUESTION MARK
pupa

COMMA
pupa

ANGLE WINGS This group of small and medium-sized butterflies has angular, notched forewings. The hindwings often have short tails. Of 25 species found in this country, the question mark (also called the violet-tip), comma, and the mourning cloak (p. 69) are best known. The brownish larvae of the question mark feed on hop, elm, and nettle. The greenish, often pale comma caterpillar feeds on nettles. Both caterpillars have branched spines on each body segment.

Comma

Question Mark

MOURNING CLOAK
1.0" w. 2.6"

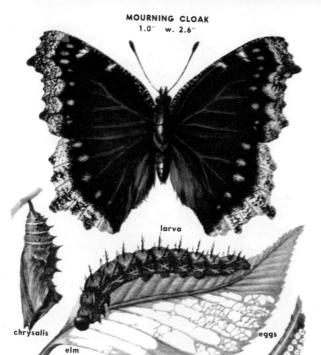

larva

chrysalis

elm

eggs

MOURNING CLOAK This butterfly, like the other angle wings, hibernates as an adult and hence makes its appearance very early in spring. Dark, barrel-shaped eggs are soon laid on twigs of poplar, elm, hackberry, or willow. The gregarious caterpillars occasionally injure a tree by stripping the foliage. The mourning cloak is common and widely distributed over the entire northern hemisphere. In the North it has one brood a year; in the South, two.

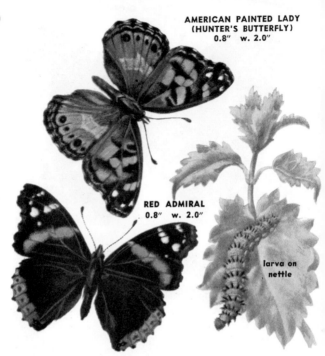

AMERICAN PAINTED LADY
(HUNTER'S BUTTERFLY)
0.8" w. 2.0"

RED ADMIRAL
0.8" w. 2.0"

larva on
nettle

RED ADMIRAL, AMERICAN PAINTED LADY, and PAINTED LADY Two of these three closely related butterflies are difficult to distinguish. But the red admiral is clear and unmistakable because of the red bands on its forewings and red borders on its hindwings. The red admiral is found the world around in the northern hemisphere. The light green eggs are barrel-shaped. The caterpillar feeds on hops, ramie, and nettles. American painted lady is restricted to North America. Its upper side is very similar to that of the painted lady. The under side is distinct

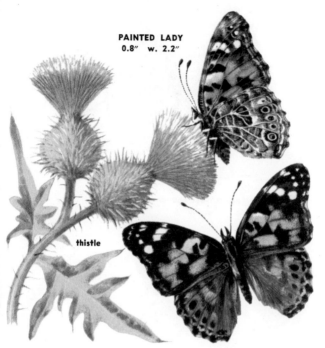

PAINTED LADY
0.8" w. 2.2"

thistle

in having two large "eye-spots" which the painted lady lacks. The American's larvae are spiny and black, with rows of white spots. It feeds on arrowweed, cudweed, and other everlastings. The painted lady or thistle butterfly is reported to be the most widely distributed of all known butterflies. This may be because burdock, thistles, sunflowers, nettles, and other plants which larvae eat are widely distributed also. Caterpillar is greenish, with black spots and light, branched spines.

Red Admiral
and
Painted Lady

Amer. Painted Lady

EYED BROWN
0.6″ w. 1.8″

PEARLY-EYE and larva
0.7″ w. 2.0″

NYMPHS AND SATYRS About 60 species make up this large group of small to medium-sized butterflies, most of which are dull brownish or gray in color. Their characteristic markings are eye-spots on the under sides of the wings. Most prefer open woods and mountain areas, generally in the north. The caterpillars of these species are smooth, and taper toward both the head and the tail, which is always forked. The larvae of the eyed brown have a pair of red horns at each end. Their food is grass and sedge. The pearly-eye is slightly larger in size, and its

COMMON WOOD NYMPH
0.8″ w. 2.0″

LITTLE WOOD SATYR
0.7″ w. 1.8″

larvae similar in appearance. The common wood nymph has a pair of yellow patches on each forewing surrounding the purplish eye-spots. The male has two small eye-spots on the hindwings. Markings vary a good deal. The larvae lack the horns of the first two species. The little wood satyr is smaller, with eye-spots on both fore- and hindwings. It prefers open forests and thickets. The larva has no red at all; its color varies from greenish to pale brown. It, too, feeds on grasses.

Wood Nymph

Pearly Eye

GRAY HAIRSTREAK
0.4" w. 1.2"

PURPLISH COPPER
0.5" w. 1.2"

AMERICAN COPPER
0.4" w. 1.0"

BRONZE COPPER
0.5" w. 1.5"

COPPERS AND BLUES This large family of small butterflies includes over 2,000 species, but not many species are found in this country. These butterflies are common. The family has three groups. The hairstreaks are usually brownish or bluish, with hair-like tails at the tip of the hindwings. About 60 species of hairstreaks live in the United States. The second group, the coppers, are nearly all a copper-red color with black markings. There are some 18 species. The American copper is probably our most common butterfly. It is found everywhere east of the Rockies. The last group, the blues, are very small. Western

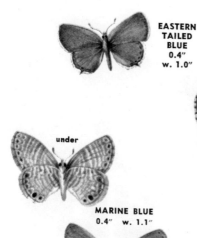

EASTERN TAILED BLUE
0.4″ w. 1.0″

SPRING AZURE
0.4″ w. 1.1″

under

MARINE BLUE
0.4″ w. 1.1″

upper

WESTERN PYGMY BLUE
0.2″ w. 0.6″

pygmy blue, with a wingspread of a bit over ½ inch, is our smallest butterfly. Blues are more common in the West. Some 40 species, variable in form and difficult to identify, are listed for the United States. The spring azure has over 13 different variations. The caterpillars of all this family are short, thick, and slug-like. Some are flattened and covered with fine hair. They feed on a variety of plants including oak, hickory, hops, and sorrel. One species has a carnivorous caterpillar which devours plant lice.

Eastern Tailed Blue

Gray Hairstreak

Amer. Copper

CABBAGE BUTTERFLY
0.7" w. 1.8"

larva

chrysalis

CABBAGE BUTTERFLY This all-too-common species ranges over most of the northern hemisphere. It first entered this country in 1868 and within 20 years had spread to the Rockies. Now these insects are found in every cabbage field; the green caterpillars feed also on mustard and related wild plants. Two or three broods mature each year, the last brood hibernating as the chrysalis and emerging in early spring. Adults often fly in flocks of a dozen or two.

COMMON SULPHUR
0.8" w. 2.0"

ALFALFA BUTTERFLY
0.8" w. 2.1"

alfalfa

COMMON larva

SULPHURS

Dozens of common or clouded sulphurs hover as a yellow cloud over roadside puddles. Their color is variable; females are paler, with yellow spots in borders of forewings. There are two generations annually. The alfalfa butterfly, also varying in color, is sometimes pale. It also is common along roadsides, in fields and gardens. The larva is similar to the common sulphur's, but has pink stripes. Both these larvae feed on clover, alfalfa, and other legumes.

Alfalfa Butterfly

Common Sulphur

SPICEBUSH SWALLOWTAIL
0.8″   w. 3.5″

PARNASSIUS
0.8″   w. 2.4″

GIANT SWALLOWTAIL
1.0″   w. 4.4″

ZEBRA SWALLOWTAIL
0.8" w. 2.7"

BLACK SWALLOWTAIL 0.8" w. 2.8"

TIGER SWALLOWTAIL
0.9" w. 3.8"

SWALLOWTAILS Here are our largest and most attractive butterflies. Over 20 species occur in the United States and many others are found elsewhere, making the swallowtails a group that is widely known, admired, collected, and studied. Closely related to the swallowtails are the parnassians, more common in the West. These lack the "tail" on the hindwings that gives the swallowtails their name. The caterpillars pupate on the ground. The mountain butterfly is an example of this group.

The swallowtails are predominantly black or yellow. Some species occur in several forms. The female tiger swallowtail may be either yellow or black, the black form being more common in the South. Swallowtail eggs are usually round, flattened at the base. The caterpillars are generally smooth, lacking spines, though the pipevine swallowtails have fleshy horns (p. 81). All the larvae can emit a rather strong, musky odor which may protect them. The chrysalis rests on its tail end, supported by a loop of silk at the middle. There are often two broods a year.

The swallowtails illustrated here are easy to identify in spite of variations in color. Their caterpillars and food plants are shown on the next page. The zebra swallowtail has the longest tail of any native species. The giant swallowtail is the largest, with a spread of 4 to 5½ inches. It is most common in the Southeast. Its larvae are occasionally destructive to citrus orchards. Both male and female black swallowtail have a double row of yellow spots, but those of the female are smaller. Yellow spots on the forewings and greenish hindwings mark the spicebush swallowtail. The pipevine swallowtail lacks the yellow spots.

SPICEBUSH on sassafras

ZEBRA on pawpaw

PIPEVINE on pipevine

BLACK on parsley

GIANT on orange

TIGER on wild cherry

SWALLOWTAIL CATERPILLARS
and their food plants

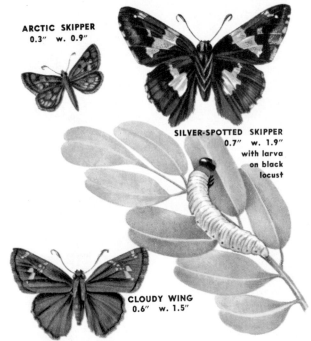

ARCTIC SKIPPER
0.3" w. 0.9"

SILVER-SPOTTED SKIPPER
0.7" w. 1.9"
with larva
on black
locust

CLOUDY WING
0.6" w. 1.5"

SKIPPERS About 200 kinds of skippers are native, and this is only one-tenth of the total number. Their rapid, darting flight gives them their name. These small butterflies have characteristics of moths. Some rest with the hindwings or both wings horizontal as moths do. The smooth caterpillars have large heads and thin "necks." They feed on locust, clover, and other plants. The silver-spotted skipper is the most common of the large skippers. Many are much smaller than this.

Silver-spotted Skipper

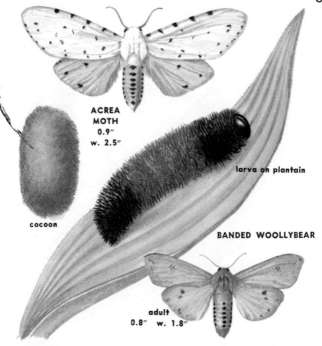

ACREA
MOTH
0.9"
w. 2.5"

larva on plantain

cocoon

BANDED WOOLLYBEAR

adult
0.8" w. 1.8"

ACREA MOTHS and BANDED WOOLLYBEARS represent a family of some 200 American species. Acrea is one of the most common eastern moths, easily identified by the spotted abdomen. The male is illustrated. The female's hindwings are white. Caterpillars feed on grasses and garden plants. The banded woollybear or Isabella moth caterpillar, abundant in autumn, feeds on plantain and related plants. It hibernates as larva and pupates in spring. Both larvae use hair in making cocoons.

Acrea Moth and
Banded Woollybear

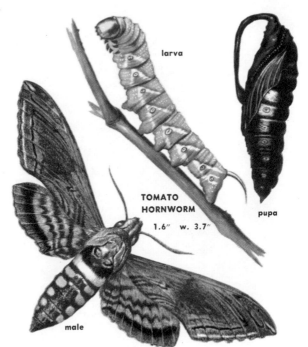

larva

pupa

TOMATO HORNWORM

1.6" w. 3.7"

male

SPHINX MOTHS Some 100 species of these thick-bodied, narrow-winged moths live in this country. Their common names, as tomato worm and tobacco worm, indicate the foods sought by some larvae. Leaves, and sometimes fruits, are eaten. Some larvae feed on potatoes and on wild members of the potato family. Other species eat birch, willow, catalpa, grape, and other plants, occasionally damaging nurseries and vineyards. The larvae are large and usually have a tail or horn. Some rear back into a belligerent attitude when molested, but none are poisonous, as is sometimes believed. Braconid

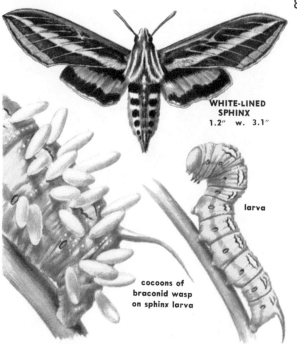

**WHITE-LINED
SPHINX**
1.2" w. 3.1"

larva

cocoons of
braconid wasp
on sphinx larva

wasps lay their eggs in the living caterpillars, which the wasp larvae eat. Caterpillars of Sphinx moths covered with wasp cocoons are often seen. Caterpillars pupate in the ground, and some may be recognized by the free tongue case, which forms a loop at one end. The common adults are identified by abdominal or wing markings. The sucking-tube mouth is long, enabling Sphinx moths to get nectar and pollinate tubular flowers, such as nicotina, petunia, honeysuckle, and trumpet vine.

Tomato Hornworm
and White-lined Sphinx

AILANTHUS SILK MOTH
1.0″ w. 4.2″

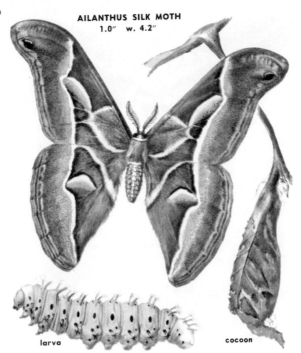

larva

cocoon

AILANTHUS SILK MOTH This moth was imported from China, where a coarse grade of silk is obtained from its cocoons. Since 1861 it has become firmly established in the East. The silk industry, which it was hoped this moth would start, never materialized. The large caterpillars are controlled by natural enemies, and since they feed chiefly on ailanthus, a weed tree, they are not harmful. These are the only large moths with white tufts on the abdomen.

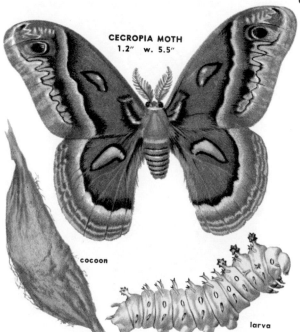

CECROPIA MOTH
1.2″ w. 5.5″

cocoon

larva

CECROPIA MOTH The large, tubercle-studded cecropia larvae feed on cherry, maple, willow, and many other plants. The large, tough, brown cocoons are firmly attached to branches and are easily found in winter. Outdoors, the huge moths emerge in late spring or summer, but when cocoons are brought indoors they hatch earlier. The emergence of the adult is a sight to see. The wrinkled, velvety wings unfold till they are 5 or 6 inches across—something worth watching!

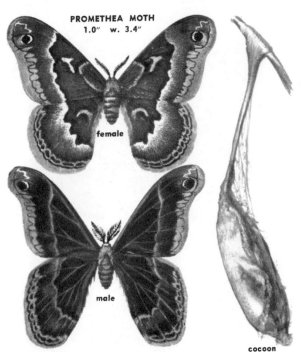

PROMETHEA MOTH
1.0" w. 3.4"

female

male

cocoon

PROMETHEA MOTH This moth, sometimes called the spicebush silk moth, has a bluish-green larva with two pairs of short red horns near the head. It feeds on sassafras, wild cherry, tulip tree, and sweet gum, as well as on spicebush. Collect the compact cocoons, each wrapped in a dry leaf, and watch the adults emerge in spring. Recognize the male by its darker maroon color. The female is a bit larger, lighter, and browner, with slightly different markings.

larva

cocoon

POLYPHEMUS MOTH
1.3" w. 5.3"

POLYPHEMUS MOTH Because of its gigantic size and the "eye-spots" on the wings, this night-flying silk moth was named after the one-eyed giant, Polyphemus, of Greek mythology. The green larvae, sometimes over 3 inches long, feed on oak, hickory, elm, maple, birch, and other trees and shrubs. They spin their plump cocoons either on the ground or attached to a twig. These moths are more common in the South, where there are two broods a year.

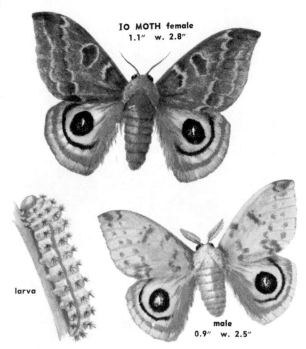

IO MOTH female
1.1" w. 2.8"

larva

male
0.9" w. 2.5"

IO MOTHS Three very similar species are found in this country. The larvae are of particular interest, for their sharp spines are mildly poisonous. Recognize them by their horizontal red-and-white stripe. Handle them with care when you find them—on corn and other garden and wild plants. Ichneumon flies (p. 137) often attack the larvae. The cocoon is found on the ground in dead leaves. The adult male is smaller than the female and has bright yellow forewings.

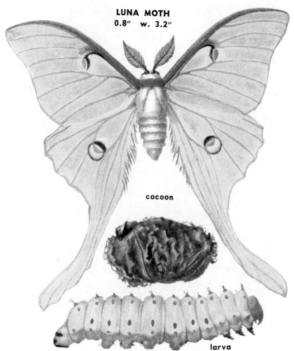

LUNA MOTH
0.8″ w. 3.2″

cocoon

larva

LUNA MOTH This handsome moth, with its striking long tails and delicate green color, makes a lasting impression on those who see it for the first time. It is a favorite with collectors of moths and butterflies. The larvae, smaller than the other night-fliers, feed on sweet gum, walnut, hickory, and persimmon. The cocoons are usually spun on the ground. Male and female are similar in appearance. Some have more purple on the borders of the wings than others.

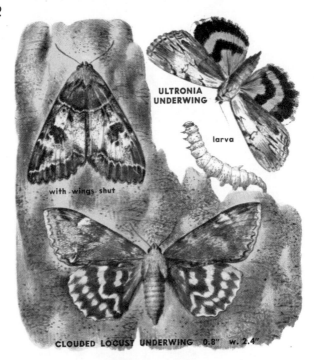

ULTRONIA UNDERWING

larva

with wings shut

CLOUDED LOCUST UNDERWING 0.8" w. 2.4"

UNDERWING MOTHS There are over 100 species of these attractive moths in the United States, and a variety of underwings can be found in every locality. Collect them in woods at night after painting tree trunks and stumps with a mixture of brown sugar and fermented fruit juice as bait. When the adult rests on bark with its wings folded, it can scarcely be seen. In flight, the bright colors of the underwings are in sharp contrast to the drab pattern of the forewings.

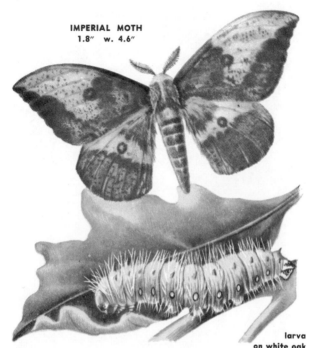

IMPERIAL MOTH
1.8″ w. 4.6″

larva
on white oak

IMPERIAL AND REGAL MOTHS These moths are
closely related to the large silk moths. The hairy imperial
caterpillar, with short horns near the head, varies from
green to brown. It feeds on pine, hickory, oak, maple,
and other trees. No cocoon is formed, the pupa resting in
the ground. The forewings of the male are purplish; those
of the female are richer in yellows.
The larvae of regal moths, which
feed on walnuts, have large, red,
curved horns.

Imperial

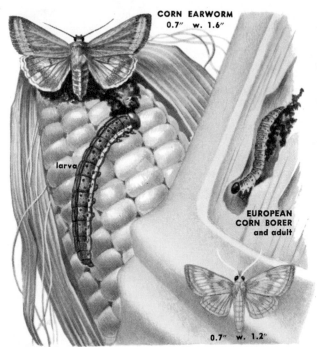

CORN EARWORM
0.7" w. 1.6"

larva

EUROPEAN
CORN BORER
and adult

0.7" w. 1.2"

CORN EARWORM AND BORERS Everyone who has husked sweet corn has seen the greenish or brown larva of the corn earworm, found almost everywhere. It feeds on other garden crops, too, and pupates underground. The European corn borer became established near Boston in 1917 and has spread widely since, doing millions of dollars' damage to corn. The larvae bore into stalks, weakening and breaking them. Control is difficult, as borers live in wild plants also.

European
Corn Borer

Corn Earworm

wingless
female

male 0.5"   w. 1.4"

WHITE-MARKED TUSSOCK MOTH   The larvae, often
seen in late summer, are recognized by their tufted
white hairs and attractive contrasting colors. They are
pests of most shade and ornamental trees and are best
controlled by destroying cocoons in winter. The egg
masses are laid by the wingless females on the surface of
their cocoons. Eggs hatch in spring,
but the larvae are not noticeable
till summer. Adults are small and in-
conspicuous.

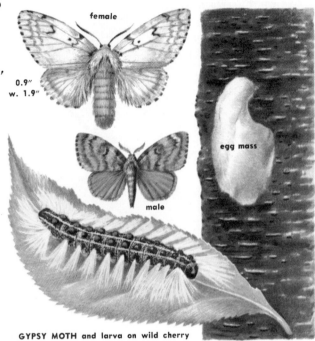

female

0.9"
w. 1.9"

egg mass

male

GYPSY MOTH and larva on wild cherry

GYPSY MOTH The gypsy and the brown-tail moth are European relatives of the white-marked tussock moth which, unfortunately, have become established in this country. The larvae, somewhat similar to tussock moths, without tussocks, eat the leaves of most shade and forest trees. They tend to feed at night. Larvae pupate in mid-summer and adults emerge shortly. The female flies but little. She lays a mass of eggs, covering them with hair and scales. These hatch in spring.

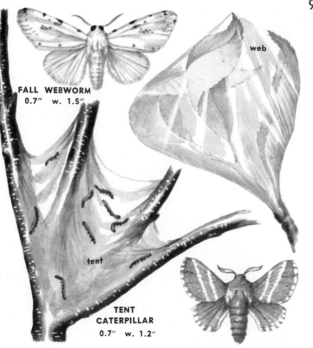

FALL WEBWORM
0.7"   w. 1.5"

web

tent

TENT
CATERPILLAR
0.7"   w. 1.2"

TENT CATERPILLARS AND FALL WEBWORMS

These two pests of forest, shade, and ornamental trees are not closely related, but are often confused. Both build webs, but that of the fall webworm covers the leaves. The tent caterpillar web, built only in spring, is usually at the crotch of branches. Adult webworms, with variable black spots on forewings, lay eggs on leaves. Tent caterpillar egg masses are found on twigs. Remove them in winter to control this insect.

Tent Caterpillar
and Fall Webworm

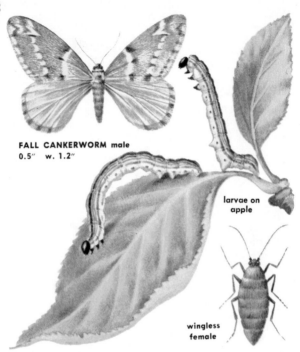

FALL CANKERWORM male
0.5" w. 1.2"

larvae on
apple

wingless
female

CANKERWORMS These pests of apple, other fruit, and shade trees are worth watching as they lope along on their true and false legs. Sometimes they spin a silken thread and hang suspended in mid-air. Fall and spring cankerworms are equally obnoxious. The wingless females lay their eggs on bark. After feasting on leaves, the larvae pupate underground. The adults emerge late in fall and can be trapped by bands of sticky paper around tree trunks.

Fall Cankerworm

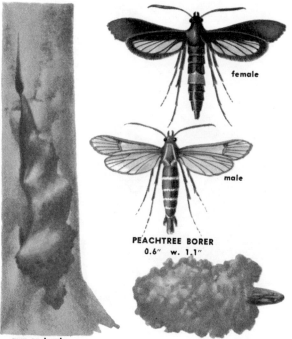

female

male

PEACHTREE BORER
0.6" w. 1.1"

gum on trunk

cocoon

PEACHTREE BORER larvae enter the tree as soon as they hatch from the eggs, which have been laid on the bark. The larvae burrows can be recognized by exuding gum on the surface. After spending the winter as a larva, the borer pupates in a crude cocoon. The adult emerges in about a month and mates. The female lays a new mass of several hundred eggs. This pest is a native insect which is believed to have fed on wild plum and cherry before peaches were introduced.

CODLING MOTH
0.4" w. 0.8"

larva in apple

CODLING MOTH This pest is so widespread that spraying apple trees for its control is a routine operation. Introduced from Europe, the codling moth is now widely distributed. Tiny eggs are deposited on leaves. As they hatch, the larvae enter the new fruit. Later, larvae hatch from eggs laid on the apples. After feeding in the fruit, larvae pupate on the bark. There are often several generations a year. Late larvae hibernate and pupate the following spring.

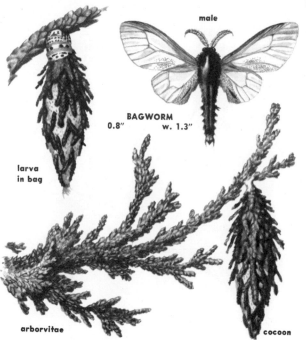

male

BAGWORM
0.8"   w. 1.3"

larva
in bag

arborvitae

cocoon

BAGWORMS are common but become serious pests only locally. Their life history is strange. The wingless and footless female, after mating, crawls back into her "bag" and lays hundreds of yellow eggs, which hatch in spring. The young larvae feed on leaves of many kinds of trees, building their conical bags as they feed. Later they bind their bags to twigs and pupate. The male emerges, seeks the female, and mates. Several related moths make bags which are similar in design.

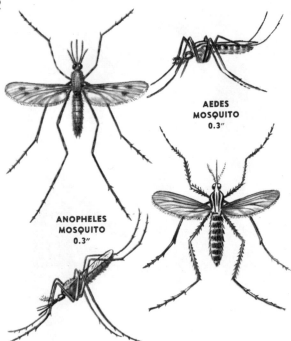

**AEDES
MOSQUITO
0.3"**

**ANOPHELES
MOSQUITO
0.3"**

MOSQUITOES   This large group of small but important insects has been amply studied as part of public-health campaigns against malaria and yellow fever. The conquest of malaria is a scientific milestone. The common carriers of the disease, the anopheles mosquitoes, are recognized by the "three-pronged" beak of the female and by the tilted position they assume when resting. The aedes mosquitoes, one of which carries yellow fever, are more like the common house and swamp mosquito in appearance. The disease carrier is limited to tropics and

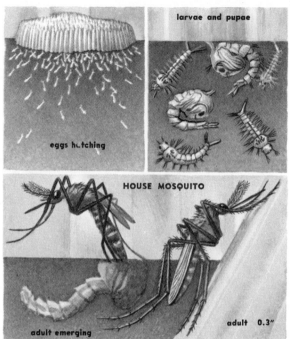

larvae and pupae

eggs hatching

HOUSE MOSQUITO

adult emerging

adult 0.3"

subtropics. Female culex mosquitoes lay rafts of several hundred eggs, which hatch in a few days into larval wrigglers. In a week or so these pupate, and the adults soon emerge. Male mosquitoes are harmless. Their beaks are not fitted for piercing. Females bite and hence can transmit disease. They are the only ones which buzz. Mosquitoes have been controlled by draining swamps and by the wide use of insecticides. The possibility of long-range dangers in these methods, particularly when applied by inadequately informed persons, needs further study.

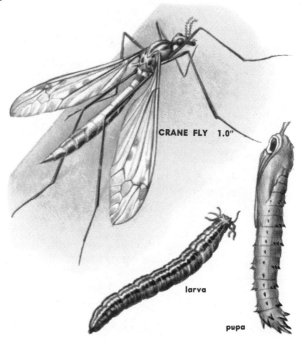

CRANE FLY 1.0"

larva

pupa

CRANE FLIES Adult crane flies are sometimes mistaken for giant mosquitoes. But the adults, often seen around electric lights, may not eat at all. Some are apparently predaceous. The female lays several hundred eggs on damp soil. The larvae burrow into the ground or decaying wood. Only a few attack plants. In a few weeks they pupate, and in about a week appear as adults. Crane flies form a large group, with over 1000 species in this country.

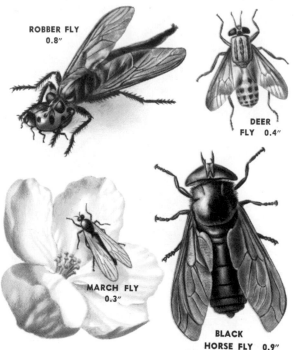

ROBBER FLY
0.8"

DEER
FLY 0.4"

MARCH FLY
0.3"

BLACK
HORSE FLY 0.9"

FLIES include serious pests of plants and animals which cause losses running into millions. The vast majority are harmless; some species are beneficial. The robber fly preys on insects, some larger than itself. The deer fly and the black fly can make a camper miserable. March flies (which are more common late in spring) are often seen on flowers. The black horse fly, sometimes a full inch long, bites severely. Many flies transmit disease as they bite infected animals and then others. Insect repellents and insecticides are useful in controlling them.

BLUEBOTTLE FLY 0.5"

larva

**GREENBOTTLE FLY
0.5"**

pupa

BLUEBOTTLE AND GREENBOTTLE FLIES are attractive insects, but thoroughly obnoxious otherwise. Eggs are laid on dead animals, garbage, sewage, or in open wounds of animals. Some related species parasitize and kill animals and even man. Eggs hatch very soon after being laid; larvae are mature in less than 2 weeks. The short life cycle means several generations a season; only continual spraying will keep these pests under control.

Bluebottle
and Greenbottle

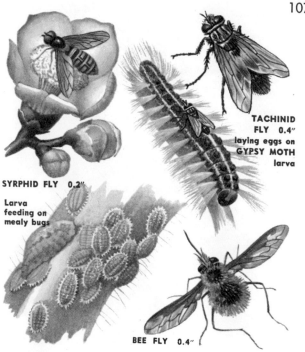

SYRPHID FLY 0.2"

Larva feeding on mealy bugs

TACHINID FLY 0.4" laying eggs on GYPSY MOTH larva

BEE FLY 0.4"

TACHINID AND OTHER FLIES Tachinid flies are beneficial insects which help control injurious ones. More than 1,400 species have been described. Because these flies are prolific, their value as parasites is increased. Syrphid flies, known as flower or drone flies, are similar insects. They are often seen approaching a flower, coming to an abrupt stop and hovering in mid-air. The larvae eat aphids and scales. The fuzzy, squat bee fly lives in hives, and its larvae often attack and feed on larvae of bees and other insects.

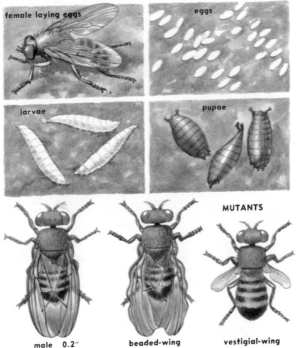

female laying eggs

eggs

larvae

pupae

MUTANTS

male 0.2"   beaded-wing   vestigial-wing

FRUIT FLY These small and rather important flies are often seen around rotting or fermenting fruit. Their claim to fame rests on scientific uses to which they have been put. Fruit flies have been used in hundreds of experiments dealing with inheritance. They have probably been studied from this angle more intensely than any other animal. The fact that their life cycle is less than 2 weeks enhances their value in this work. They are easily grown in the laboratory, where interesting forms have appeared naturally or from exposure to experimental radiation.

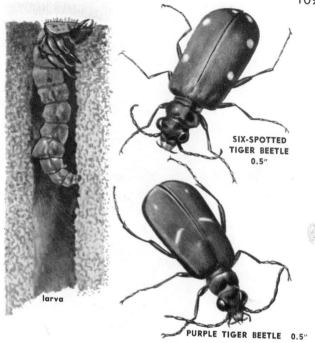

SIX-SPOTTED
TIGER BEETLE
0.5"

PURPLE TIGER BEETLE 0.5"

larva

TIGER BEETLES These handsome beetles are often seen on summer afternoons darting in and out of paths. They are widely distributed and quite common, but agile, swift, and difficult to catch. Eggs are laid in the soil. The predatory larvae, locally called "doodlebugs," dig deep burrows and wait at the openings to catch passing insects in their powerful jaws. Some tiger beetles living on beaches or other sandy areas are protectively colored gray.

Six-spotted

ROSE CHAFER 0.4"

ROSE CHAFER This slim, hairy beetle is one of the many scarab beetles, a large family of over 30,000 species, diverse in size and appearance. Some are important pests. The rose chafer feeds on roses, grapes, and a variety of other plants. Adults appear in late spring and early summer, eating both leaves and flowers. The larvae burrow into the ground, where they feed on roots, especially those of grasses. Control of the rose chafer is difficult.

Rose Chafer

Related forms

JAPANESE BEETLE 0.4"

JAPANESE BEETLE When these Japanese insects were first discovered on plants in New Jersey in 1916, experts could scarcely find a dozen. Now thousands can be collected daily, and control is a serious problem. The small, white grubs feed on the roots of grasses, damaging lawns. The larvae dig deep for winter and pupate the following spring. The adults emerge in midsummer and feed on cultivated plants and fruits. After mating, eggs are deposited in soil.

112

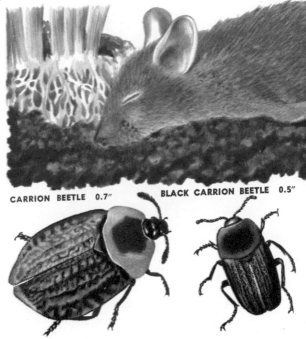

CARRION BEETLE 0.7"   BLACK CARRION BEETLE 0.5"

CARRION AND ROVE BEETLES form a family of over 100 species, in two groups: the carrion and the burying beetles. The former are smaller, flattened insects which, as scavengers, feed on decaying animal matter. Some kinds are predators, feeding on worms and insects; a few eat plants. Both larvae and adults have similar feeding habits. It is reported that the larger burying beetles, some brightly colored, dig under the carcass of a small animal till it falls into the hole

Burying Beetles

Related species

AMERICAN BURYING BEETLES 1.2"

HAIRY BURYING BEETLE 0.7"   HAIRY ROVE BEETLE 0.8"

and is actually buried to serve as food for the larvae. The eggs are deposited on the corpse. The larvae of some species develop rapidly, reaching maturity in about a week. Rove beetles, which are also scavengers or predators, have short wing-covers and superficially resemble the earwigs (p. 29). They are a larger group—over 1,000 species are reported for this country. Some live in fungi or in ants' nests. Some squirt a malodorous mist or droplet at enemies.

Hairy Rove Beetle and Carrion Beetles

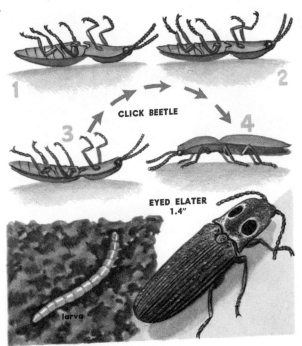

CLICK BEETLE

EYED ELATER
1.4"

larva

CLICK BEETLES form a family of some 500 American species. The eyed elater is a striking example. If it falls or lands on its back, it lies quietly for perhaps a minute. Then, with a loud click, it flips into the air. If it is lucky, it lands on its feet and runs away; otherwise it tries again. The larvae of click beetles, known as wireworms, live in the ground or in rotten wood. Most click-beetle larvae feed on roots, injuring potatoes and other crops. Some eat other insects.

Click Beetles

Eyed
Elater

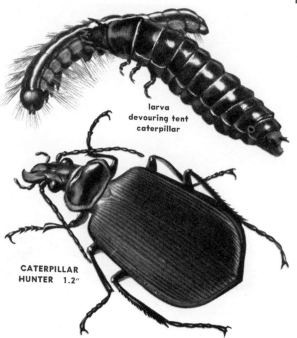

larva
devouring tent
caterpillar

CATERPILLAR
HUNTER 1.2"

CATERPILLAR HUNTERS are a group of fairly large and very attractive beetles. The family to which they belong is also large (some 2,000 American species) and is related to the tiger beetles (p. 109). These beetles are all predaceous, feeding on insects and other small animals. Larvae of the caterpillar hunters attack and feed on caterpillars of the gypsy moth and tent caterpillars. Some adults squirt an acrid fluid on their victims or on unwary collectors.

FIREFLIES 0.5"

FIREFLIES are not flies at all, but soft-bodied beetles, and most unusual insects. About 50 species are known in this country, and many more, even more marvelous, are found widely distributed in the tropics. The light-giving property, or luminescence, is not confined to the adults. In some species the eggs and larvae glow also. The females of some species are wingless: these are known as glowworms. Fireflies are of little economic importance. They add to the pleasure of a summer's night: the tropical display of thousands of these insects flashing in unison is breathtaking. Fireflies have posed a problem which scientists have not yet solved—that of "cold" light. The study of this phenomenon may have wide practical ap-

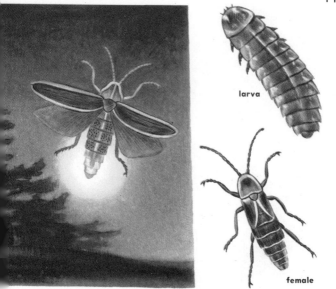

larva

female

plications. In the species shown, it is the last segment of the abdomen which contains the light-producing tissue. This is very fatty and includes a network of nerves and airtubes. Through the latter, oxygen for the light-producing process is obtained. In ordinary rapid oxidation much more heat than light is produced; here, heat production is negligible.

The larvae live underground or in rotted wood or rubbish. They feed on small insects. The adults are reported to eat the same food, but some of the common fireflies may not feed at all in the adult stage. Put some in a jar and watch the action.

Glowworm

Other Fireflies

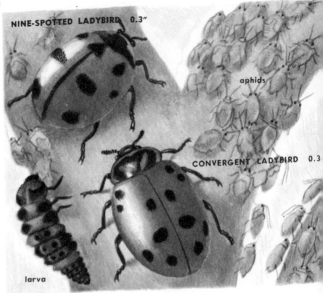

NINE-SPOTTED LADYBIRD 0.3"

aphids

CONVERGENT LADYBIRD 0.3

larva

LADYBIRD BEETLES are probably the best known and most valued of our beetles. We have some 350 species in this country, though the family is world-wide in distribution. Lutz says the name can be traced back to the Middle Ages, when these beetles were dedicated to the Virgin—hence the name ladybird or ladybug. Both larvae and adults of many species feed on aphids. In California, where these pests and scale insects cause serious damage to citrus trees, native and imported ladybird beetles have been successfully used to hold the pests in check. When the cottony-cushion scale from Australia (pp. 40-41) began to spread through California orange groves, the entire industry was threatened. An Australian ladybug

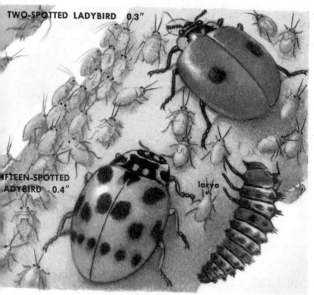

TWO-SPOTTED LADYBIRD 0.3"

FIFTEEN-SPOTTED LADYBIRD 0.4"

larva

which feeds entirely on the scale was imported and within a few years the scale was under control. About 3,000 beetles will protect an acre of trees. The common species are generally similar in appearance but differ in the number of spots. All have very short legs, which distinguish these beetles from other garden beetles (pp. 120-125). Ladybird beetles lay their eggs on plants infected with aphids or scales. The larvae feed on the aphids and pass through four growth stages. When mature, they pupate in the remains of the last larval skin. Adults assemble by the thousands before cold weather sets in and hibernate under fallen branches or rocks.

Other Ladybirds

15-spotted Ladybird

GARDEN BEETLES

Garden beetles are pests of the garden as well as the farm. They are the ones we spray, dust, and pick. Other beetles are destructive in the garden also, as the May beetle, Japanese beetle, and several weevils. These beetles illustrate the point that any cultivated crop is a banquet for the right plant-eating insects. It takes eternal vigilance to keep our cultivated plants healthy and unspoiled for our own use.

MEXICAN BEAN BEETLE is related to the common ladybird, and is one of the fairly large group of the ladybird family that feed on plants. Eggs are laid on the undersides of leaves. Spiny, yellow larvae eat the soft leaf tissue, leaving the veins behind. They eat pods too, stripping a plant in short order. Adults have similar feeding habits. Bean beetles feed on members of the pea family, wild and cultivated—peas, beans, alfalfa, and soybeans.

COLORADO POTATO BEETLE is an example of how a relatively unimportant insect can change its role as the environment changes. This beetle was once native to the Rockies, living on nightshade and other wild members of the potato family. When settlers began to grow potatoes, this new food gave the beetles a fresh start. They prospered and spread, till they now exist in practically all of the 48 states. Eggs are laid in clusters on the leaves, which larvae eat. Larvae pupate in the ground. The adults emerge and continue to feed on potatoes.

STRIPED BLISTER BEETLE or striped potato beetle has interesting relatives that parasitize bees. This species has a complex life history with unusual larvae. It feeds on potatoes, tomatoes, and related plants. Other species feed on goldenrod, alfalfa, clover, and other wild plants.

MEXICAN BEAN BEETLE
0.3"
eggs and
larva

122

COLORADO POTATO BEETLE

larva

adult
0.4"

eggs

STRIPED BLISTER BEETLE 0.7"

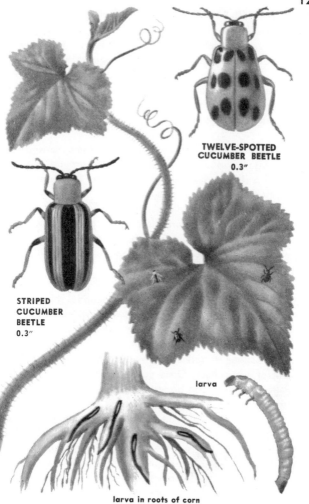

**TWELVE-SPOTTED
CUCUMBER BEETLE**
0.3"

**STRIPED
CUCUMBER
BEETLE**
0.3"

larva

larva in roots of corn

CUCUMBER BEETLES The striped and spotted cucumber beetles are common garden pests. The larvae of the former attack roots, and the adults eat leaves of cucumber, squash, and related plants. The 12-spotted cucumber beetle is an even worse pest, feeding on many other plants besides those of the squash family. It appears early in the season and stays late. In the South, the larvae attack the roots of corn, oats, and other grasses.

ASPARAGUS BEETLES, two species of them, ravage the asparagus crop. Adults hibernate in the ground, emerging in spring to feed on young shoots. Eggs are soon laid and larvae attack shoots, "leaves," and fruit, stripping the plant. The life cycle takes only about a month, so there are several broods a year. Both species, the common asparagus beetle and the spotted asparagus beetle, were introduced from Europe, one about 90, and the other about 70, years ago.

CONTROL OF GARDEN PESTS Control of garden insects first requires a knowledge of which pests are involved and something of their eating habits. If you cannot identify the insect, seek aid of your county agent, college of agriculture, museum, or the U.S. Department of Agriculture. Once you know the insect, proper control measures can be learned from the same sources. State and Federal agricultural agencies have pamphlets on control of garden pests. The

pamphlets are available (usually free or at a nominal cost) upon request. Methods of pest control are being constantly changed to meet new conditions.

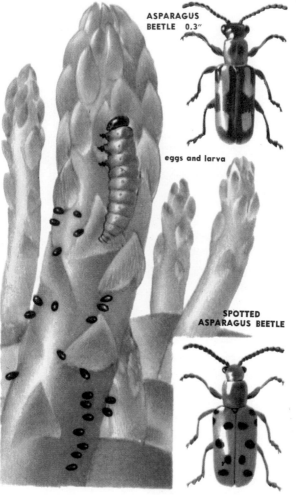

ASPARAGUS
BEETLE 0.3"

eggs and larva

SPOTTED
ASPARAGUS BEETLE

WHIRLIGIG BEETLES 0.6"

WATER SCAVENGER 1.3"

WATER BEETLES are not to be confused with water bugs (pp. 48-49), though they are found in the same habitat. The whirligig beetles, true to their name, whirl or swim at the surface. They dive when disturbed and are good fliers also. Eggs are laid on water plants; larvae feed on water animals. Eggs of diving beetles are deposited in the tissues of water plants. They hatch into larvae commonly known as water tigers, which attack water insects, small fish, and even one another. After a month or so, larvae pupate in the ground. Adults are active all year. Their

DIVING BEETLE 1.1"

MAYFLY larva

DIVING BEETLE larva

method of carrying a bubble of air down with them at the tip of their abdomen is interesting to watch.

These and other water insects can be kept in an aquarium and fed bits of meat. The water scavengers, the largest water beetles, are sometimes over 3 inches long. Eggs are laid in a silken wrapping, attached to a floating leaf. The predaceous larvae feed like those of diving beetles. Pupae form in soil by late summer, and emerge in about 2 weeks. Adults also are active in all seasons. They carry air as a film on the underside of the body.

128

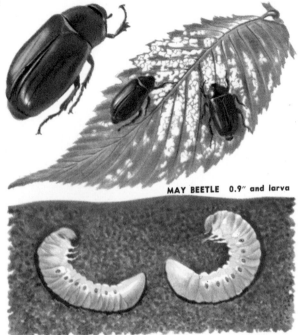

MAY BEETLE 0.9" and larva

MAY BEETLES or June bugs form a group of over 100 American species, widely distributed and difficult to control. White eggs are laid in an earth-covered ball amid roots on which the white grubs feed for 2 or 3 years. These pupate underground in fall, and adults appear the following spring. Adults feed on leaves of many common trees. They are attracted to electric lights. Birds and small mammals, such as skunks and even pigs, root out grubs and eat them.

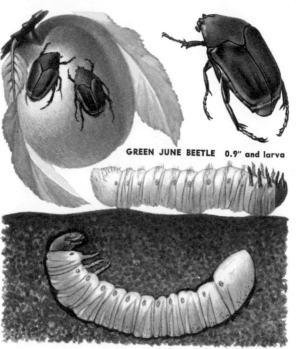

GREEN JUNE BEETLE 0.9" and larva

GREEN JUNE BEETLE Often called the figeater, this beetle feeds on many plants, eating roots, stems, and leaves. Larvae are found in soil or manure. They move by bristles on their backs instead of by their short legs. Adults fly in large numbers, making a loud buzzing which is somewhat similar to the buzzing of bumblebees. These insects are more common in the South, where the adults damage apricots, figs, grapes, melons, and other fleshy fruits.

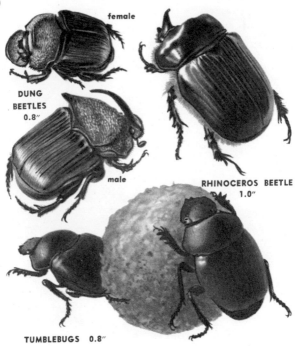

female

DUNG
BEETLES
0.8"

male

RHINOCEROS BEETLE
1.0"

TUMBLEBUGS 0.8"

SCARAB BEETLES, including the rose chafer, Japanese beetle, and May beetle, form a large family totalling more than 30,000 species, of which well over 900 are found in this country. Many are scavengers, adapted for living in or on the ground. Larvae are usually large white grubs found in the soil. Of the many scarabs, the dung beetles or tumblebugs are outstanding. These are the beetles held sacred by the Egyptians. The adults form balls of dung and roll them about giving the impression

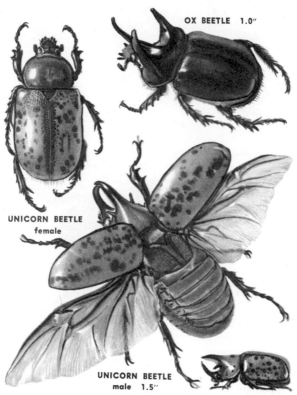

OX BEETLE 1.0"

UNICORN BEETLE
female

UNICORN BEETLE
male 1.5"

of being industrious workers. Eggs are laid in the ball, which is buried. The ferocious-looking rhinoceros beetles and their relatives, the ox beetles, are the largest of the scarabs. All are harmless. Some are 2 inches long; much larger tropical forms occur. Males have more prominent horns than females. The larvae are found in rotted wood or rich soil. Collectors prize the curious adults.

HORN BEETLE
1.4"

STAG BEETLE
male 1.6"

head of
female

STAG AND HORN BEETLES are related to scarabs. The large stags are so named because the huge mandibles of the males resemble the antlers of stags. Mouth-parts of the females are much smaller. Large white grubs are found in rotted wood—more commonly in the South than elsewhere. Horned-beetle larvae and adults are often found in large colonies in burrows in rotted logs. These beetles make noise by rubbing wing-covers or legs. The adults are harmless.

Stag

Stag

Horn

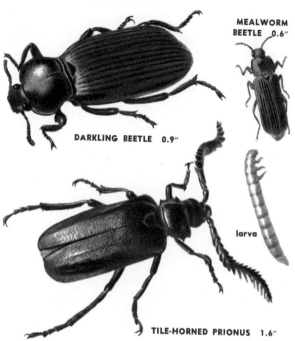

MEALWORM BEETLE 0.6"

DARKLING BEETLE 0.9"

larva

TILE-HORNED PRIONUS 1.6"

DARKLING AND PRIONUS BEETLES Darkling beetle larvae are the "mealworms" used for feeding birds and other small pets. They feed on stored grain and hence are serious pests. There are a large number of closely related species. The larvae of prionus beetles are known as round-headed borers. These attack roots of fruit and ornamental trees, grape, and other plants. The antennae, with overlapping plates, slightly longer in the male, identify the prionus beetles.

Prionus

ELDER BORER 0.8"

LOCUST BORER
0.7"

PINE SAWYER
1.0" exclusive
of antennae

FLAT-HEADED BORER 0.8"

FLAT-HEADED AND LONGHORNED BORERS Larvae
of many beetles bore into wood, but flat-headed borers
(Buprestids), like example above, and longhorned borers
(Cerambycids), represented by the locust and elder borers
and the pine sawyer, are vicious pests of orchard, shade
and forest trees. Larvae of flat-headed borers (at least 500
species in this country) feed mostly just beneath the bark,
whereas longhorned borers (over 1,000 species) usually
channel far into the trunk. The attractive locust borer adult
is often found on goldenrod.

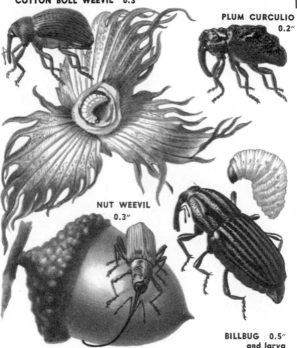

COTTON BOLL WEEVIL 0.3"

PLUM CURCULIO 0.2"

NUT WEEVIL 0.3"

BILLBUG 0.5" and larva

WEEVILS are small beetles with mouth-parts modified into a downward-curving beak or snout. Many are important pests of grain. The damage done by weevils is estimated at over $500,000,000 annually. For years, as the cotton boll weevil spread north from Mexico, warnings of the danger went unheeded. The plum curculio damages peach, cherry, and plum trees. Nut weevils are found in acorns and all other edible nuts. The granary weevils, found in grain, are prolific, with a life cycle of only 4 weeks. Some feed on the roots, others on stored grain.

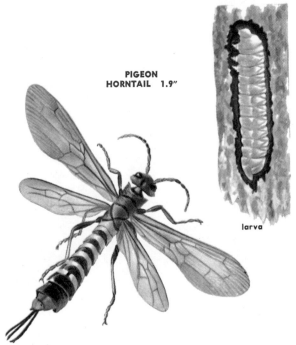

PIGEON HORNTAIL 1.9"

larva

HORNTAILS AND SAWFLIES, closely related, belong with the bees and wasps but lack the constricted abdomen. Horntails lay their eggs on dead or dying trees. The larvae are borers, which pupate in their deep tunnels. Most sawfly larvae feed on leaves. Horntails are hosts to the ichneumon flies (next page), which parasitize the larvae. The female ichneumon fly can locate a horntail burrow under several inches of wood and deposit her eggs therein.

Horntails and Sawflies

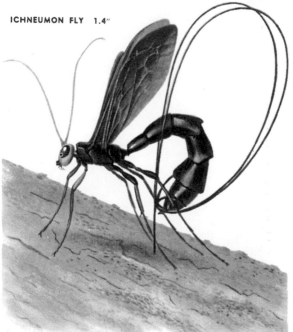

ICHNEUMON FLY 1.4"

ICHNEUMON FLIES, of which there are over 3,000 American species, play an important role in controlling many harmful insects. They are more closely related to wasps than to flies. Their larvae are parasites of cater-pillars and of larvae of beetles, flies, and other pests. The female ichneumon fly, with her unusually long ovipositor, attracts attention and is sometimes feared by those who do not know she is harmless. This ovipositor can pierce several inches of wood.

Long-tailed Ichneumon

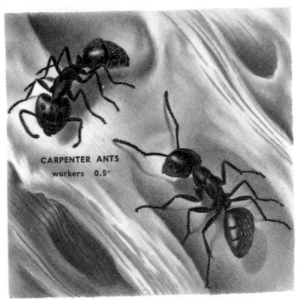

CARPENTER ANTS
workers 0.5"

CARPENTER ANTS Of over 2,500 species of ants known, all are social animals, living and working together in ways that have astonished laymen and naturalists alike. Among the most familiar of insects, they have inspired many a comparison with human society. Carpenter ants and their relatives form one of the largest groups of ants. They build nests and burrows in dead wood, logs, and the timbers of buildings, where they may do considerable damage if allowed to spread. Carpenter ants are found the world over in temperate regions. The workers, which are infertile females, are among the largest known ants.

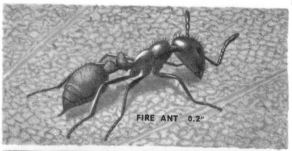

FIRE ANT 0.2"

CORNFIELD ANT 0.2"

FIRE AND CORNFIELD ANTS The fire ants of the Southeast have been known to attack baby birds and sting them to death. Cornfield ants are less ferocious and more interesting. These ants eat the sweet secretions of corn-root aphids. Aphids lay eggs in the ant burrows. When these hatch in spring, the ants place the aphids on knot-weed roots till the corn is planted and growing. Then the ants transfer the aphids to the corn roots, thus insuring a constant food supply. Cornfield ants are widely distributed and very abundant. Lutz states that they are the most abundant of all our insects, a fact which makes these small ants important.

Cornfield

Fire

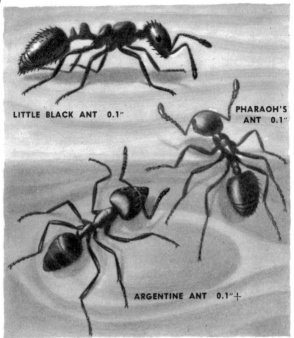

LITTLE BLACK ANT 0.1"

PHARAOH'S ANT 0.1"

ARGENTINE ANT 0.1"+

HOUSEHOLD ANTS Pharaoh's ants are small but numerous. They are common invaders of homes, feeding on any sweet foodstuffs. The Argentine ant, native to that country and Brazil, was first found in New Orleans in 1891, and has since become a serious household and garden pest in the South. They may invade nests of other ants and hives of bees. Fortunately they are semitropical and are limited in their movement northward. These ants protect aphids to secure the honey-dew they produce. Little black ants are found outdoors more than within.

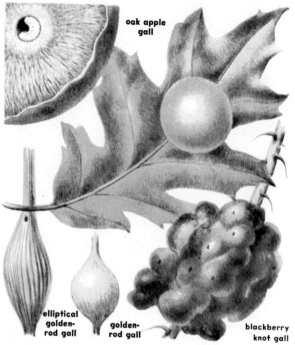

oak apple
gall

elliptical
golden-
rod gall

golden-
rod gall

blackberry
knot gall

INSECT GALLS are not well understood. Small, wasp-like insects (Cynipids), flies, and others lay eggs in plant tissues. Each insect selects a specific plant. As eggs hatch, the plant tissues around the larvae begin to swell, forming a characteristic gall. The larvae feed on plant juices and pupate in the gall. The adult emerges by burrowing through the side. Some galls are large and woody, some soft, some knobby and spiny. Best-known galls are the oak apples and the galls commonly seen on roses, blackberry, and goldenrods.

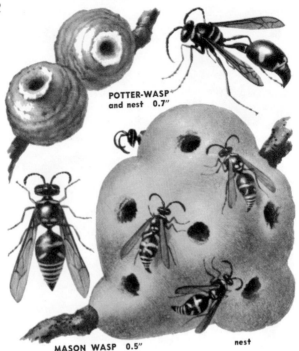

POTTER-WASP
and nest 0.7"

MASON WASP 0.5"

nest

MUD WASPS Several families of wasps are represented among those building their nests with mud. Potter-
wasps are solitary, each building a vase-shaped nest of
mud on plants. These wasps prey on caterpillars and
beetle larvae. Most mason wasps, in the same family as
the potters, nest in burrows in the soil, but the species
illustrated makes a clay nest on a branch. Best-known
mud wasps are the mud daubers, which make large nests
on walls in attics or deserted buildings. The female builds
the nest of many mud cells. In each she places several

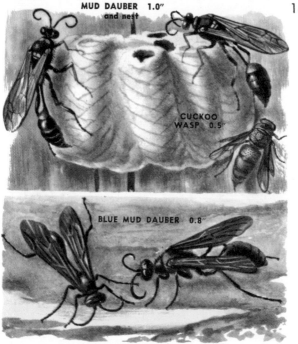

MUD DAUBER 1.0"
and nest

CUCKOO WASP 0.5"

BLUE MUD DAUBER 0.8"

paralyzed spiders or other insects before she lays the egg and seals the cell. The blue mud dauber uses nests made by the common mud dauber. The female moistens the cell wall, digs through, removes the contents, and refills the cell with her own spiders and egg. The cuckoo wasp, named after the European cuckoo, awaits its opportunity and lays its eggs in the nest of a mud dauber while the latter is off searching for a victim. The cuckoo wasp larvae feed on insects provided for the young mud dauber.

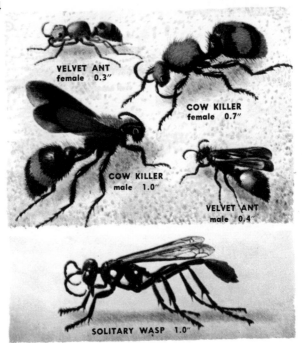

VELVET ANTS Velvet ants are so named because the wingless females are ant-like. They are parasites of wasps and bees, especially of the solitary species. The female wasp can really sting, but the males do not. The female crawls down the burrow and kills the owner with a powerful sting. She then lays her egg on the owner's larva, which her own larvae later eat. The solitary, thread-waist wasp illustrated below is one of several kinds parasitized by velvet ants.

Velvet Ants

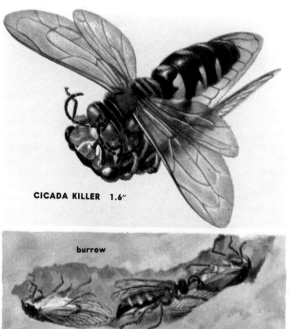

CICADA KILLER 1.6"

burrow

CICADA KILLER This large solitary wasp digs a burrow a foot or so deep. In side passages the female stores adult cicadas which she has paralyzed by stinging. The heavy cicadas are dragged up a tree by the killer till she can get enough altitude to fly back to her burrow. When the egg hatches, the larva feeds on the helpless cicada. In a week it is full grown and pupates in a loose cocoon. It emerges the following summer, completing its life cycle.

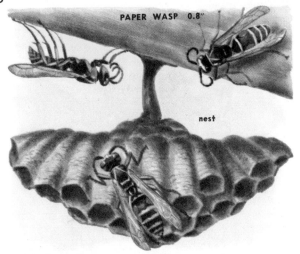

PAPER WASP 0.8"

nest

PAPER WASPS are the common wasps everyone learns to know sooner or later by painful experience. The common paper wasp builds an unprotected paper nest out of wood it chews up. The nest is hung under eaves or in barns, or in other sheltered sites. No food is placed in these nests. After the eggs hatch, the young are fed daily till they pupate. The bald-faced or white-faced hornet builds an oval, covered nest; some nests can accommodate over 10,000 hornets. Unfertilized eggs develop into drones or males. Fertilized eggs grow into workers or queens, depending on the food eaten. Queens make small brood nests in early spring. Yellow jackets, which are closely related, build nests of varying size, some underground, some hidden in rock walls or under logs. An empty fieldmouse nest is often used.

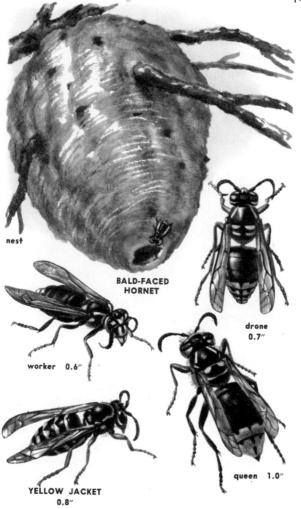

nest

BALD-FACED
HORNET

drone
0.7"

worker 0.6"

YELLOW JACKET
0.8"

queen 1.0"

BUMBLEBEE 1.0"

SWEAT BEE 0.3"

red clover

BEES are distinguished from wasps in a number of minor ways. Their legs have "pollen baskets" of stiff hairs, and the body is hairy also. Bumblebees are larger than most others. Their elongated mouth-parts enable them to pollinate red clover, which no other bee can do. Nests are made underground by the fertile females (queens), which survive the winter. The colony consists of a queen, workers, and drones. Sweat bees, small and brilliantly colored, nest in the ground. They are attracted to perspiration; hence their name. Leaf-cutting bees are larger and bright-

LEAF-CUTTING BEE 0.4"

HONEYBEE 0.5"

FLOWER BEE 0.4"

ly colored also. Their nests, made underground, are lined and divided with leaves which the bees have cut in ovals or circles from roses and other plants. The honeybee is probably the best known of all insects. Honey has been obtained from wild and from kept colonies far back into history. In making honey, bees pollinate fruit trees and other plants. A normal colony of a queen, workers, and drones may contain up to 50,000 bees. Periodically bees swarm, and the old queen goes off to found a new colony, leaving a young queen behind.

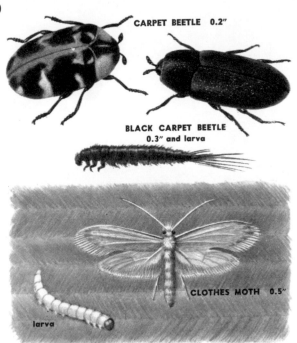

CARPET BEETLE 0.2"

BLACK CARPET BEETLE
0.3" and larva

CLOTHES MOTH 0.5"

larva

PESTS OF CLOTH AND CLOTHING The carpet
beetles are closely related to larder beetles and to
other species which destroy specimens in museums. They
eat all kinds of animal matter, thriving on rugs, woolens,
fur, leather, and hair. The larvae which do the damage
can be controlled by chemical repellents, poisons, and
sprays. Adult clothes moths do no harm. Females lay
white oval eggs on clothing, leather, etc. These hatch in
about a week into larvae, which may feed for a year on
your prized possessions before they pupate.

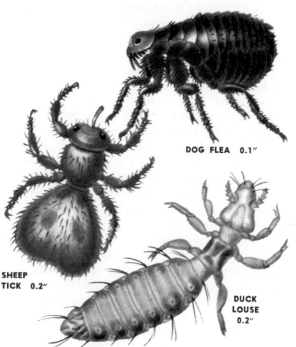

DOG FLEA 0.1"

SHEEP
TICK 0.2"

DUCK
LOUSE
0.2"

PESTS OF ANIMALS are many and cause severe losses.
Dog fleas spread from dogs to people and may, in some
areas, carry plague. They also infest other domestic animals. Control by dusting. Other species are similar. The
sheep tick, a species of fly, feeds by sucking blood. The
eggs hatch in the body of the female, and the larvae
develop to maturity before being deposited. Control is
achieved by shearing and dipping the sheep. The squalid
duck louse is typical of bird lice (not related to species on
page 32) which live on wild and domestic birds.

OTHER COMMON PESTS

Insects that do us harm have been freely scattered through the pages of this book. Some have said that these six-legged creatures are man's worst enemies. Here are more we should know to be forewarned and so forearmed.

SILVERFISH   The most primitive insect, yet still capable of eating starch from book bindings, wallpaper, and clothing. Common indoors, especially in warm places.

AMERICAN DOG TICK   No insect this: note its 4 pairs of legs. Common enough and often brought indoors after a walk through fields and woods. Check clothing and body immediately. If attached to skin, remove by touching tick with alcohol. Ticks may transmit serious virus diseases.

BEDBUG   This flat-bodied household pest, once established, may spread rapidly. May have 3 or 4 generations annually. Female lays white eggs in cracks; eggs hatch in a week or so. Destroy with DDT or other spray.

LARDER BEETLE (Dermestes)   These small beetles can be serious pests wherever food is stored. The active, hairy larvae feed on all kinds of meat, leather, and other animal products. Four or more generations are produced annually. Widely distributed in the old world and the new.

HOUSE FLY   This is the most common and most despised of all the flies. Public health campaigns have not destroyed it. Associated with garbage and filth, flies can reproduce a generation a month when temperatures are favorable. Screening, spraying with Lindane residual spray, swatting, and sanitation are recommended.

GERMAN COCKROACH or croton bug, native of Europe, has become widely established in cities. Like the silverfish it is omnivorous and damages books. Its presence does not necessarily indicate uncleanliness, and it is not a proved carrier of disease like flies. Lindane residual spray and Chlordane are recommended for control of roaches.

SILVERFISH 0.5"

AMERICAN DOG TICK 0.2"

BEDBUG 0.3"

LARDER BEETLE 0.3" and larva

HOUSE FLY 0.3"

GERMAN COCKROACH 0.6"

The study of insects requires a careful balance of what you can learn first-hand and what you can learn from others. Books and museum exhibits reflect years of research and experience of experts. Collections and field studies must be supplemented by what you read.

MUSEUMS often have systematic, habitat, and local exhibits. Curators are glad to help you identify specimens. Check colleges and universities, as well as large city and state museums. Local inquiries are always best.

BOOKS TO READ The U.S. Dept. of Agriculture and many state departments publish bulletins on insects of economic importance. Write to Supt. of Documents, Washington 25, D.C., for price list of insect bulletins. Make local inquiry for state publications. Some general books are listed below. Try them first before turning to more detailed volumes and technical reports.

Comstock, J. H., AN INTRODUCTION TO ENTOMOLOGY, Comstock Publishing Co., Ithaca, New York, 1947. A technical college text but a good systematic guide. A book for the student who wants to "get his teeth" into the subject.

Jaques, H. E., HOW TO KNOW THE INSECTS, Wm. C. Brown Co., Dubuque, Iowa, 1941. An illustrated guide to the more common orders of insects, with helpful hints on making collections. A good book for the serious amateur.

Klots, A. B., A FIELD GUIDE TO THE BUTTERFLIES, Houghton Mifflin Co., Boston, 1951. Butterflies are such a well-known and attractive group of insects that a book on them belongs in a general list. This is the best modern guide; accurate, and with color illustrations.

Lutz, Frank E., FIELD BOOK OF INSECTS, G. P. Putnam's Sons, New York, 1935. This old stand-by will aid in the identification of about 1,400 species. About half are illustrated.

Swain, Ralph, THE INSECT GUIDE, Doubleday and Co., New York, 1948. An excellent, finely illustrated book that describes the orders and principal families of insects.

Urquhart, F. A., INTRODUCING THE INSECT, Henry Holt and Co., New York, 1949. A sound "first reference," simple and non-technical, but including all common orders and families. Has easy-to-use keys as an aid to identification. Ample black-and-white illustrations.

Heavy type indicates page where species are illustrated. In scientific names the genus name is first, then the species. If the genus name is abbreviated, it is the same as the genus name preceding. The abbreviation "sp." indicates that the description applies to more than one species.

17 Diapheromera femorata.
18 Bush: Scudderia sp.
   True: Peterophylla camellifolia.
19 Microcentrum sp.
20 Mole: Gryllotalpa hexadactyla.
   Camel: Ceuthophilus sp.
21 Anabrus simplex.
22 Acheta assimilis.
23 Periplaneta americana.
24 Stagmomantis carolina.
25 Paratenodera sinensis.
26 American: Schistocerca americana.
   Carolina: Dissosteira carolina.
27 Lubber: Brachystola magna.
   Migratory: Melanoplus mexicanus.
28 Melanoplus femur-rubrum.
29 Dermaptera.
30 Isoptera.
32 Head: Pediculus humanus humanus.
   Short-nosed: Haematopinus eurysternus.
   Crab: Phthirus pubis.
   Body: Pediculus humanus corporis.
33 Ceresa bubalus.
34 Red-banded: Graphocephala coccinea.
   Lateral: Cuerna costalis.
35 Potato: Empoasca fabae.
   3-banded: Erythroneura tricincta.
   Rose: Typhlocyba rosae.
36 Magicicada septendecim.
37 Tibicen sp.
38 Philaenus sp.
39 Aphidae.
40 San Jose: Aspidiotus perniciosus.
   Terrapin: Lecanium nigrofasciatum.

41 Cottony-cushion: Icerya purchasi.
   Mealy Bug: Pseudococcus sp.
   Oystershell: Lepidosaphes ulmi.
42 Harlequin: Murgantia histrionica.
   Euschistus: Euschistus sp.
43 Shieldbug: Eurygaster alternata.
   Green Stinkbug: Acrosternum hilare.
44 Anasa tristis.
45 Small: Lygaeus kalmii.
   Large: Oncopeltus fasciatus.
46 Phymata pennsylvanica.
47 Chinch: Blissus leucopterus.
   Tarnished Plant: Lygus lineolaris.
48 Water Boatman: Corixa sp.
   Backswimmer: Notonecta sp.
49 Water Strider: Gerris sp.
   Giant Water: Lethocerus americanus.
50 Anax junius.
51 Ten-spot: Libellula pulchella.
   Blackwing: Calopteryx maculata.
52 Mayfly: Ephemerida.
   Stonefly: Plecoptera.
53 Golden-eye: Chrysopa oculata.
   Brown: Hemerobius sp.
54 Corydalus cornutus.
55 Myrmelionidae.
56 Panorpa sp.
57 Trichoptera.
60 Danaus plexippus.
61 Limenitis archippus.
62 Banded: Limenitis arthemis.
   Red-spotted: L. astyanax.
63 Precis coenia.
64 Great Spangled: Speyeria cybele.
   Meadow: Boloria toddi.
   Variegated: Euptoieta claudia.
   Regal: Speyeria idalia.

65 Gulf: Agraulis vanillae.
Silver-bordered: Boloria
myrina.
Regal: Speyeria idalia.
66 Speyeria cybele.
67 Checkerspot: Euphydryas sp.
Baltimore: E. phaëton.
68 Question Mark: Polygonia
interrogationis.
Comma: P. comma.
69 Nymphalis antiopa.
70 Amer. Painted Lady: Vanessa
virginiensis.
Red Admiral: V. atalanta.
71 Vanessa cardui.
72 Eyed Brown: Lethe eurydice.
Pearly Eye: L. portlandia.
73 Common Wood Nymph: Minois
alope.
Little Wood Satyr: Euptychia
cymela.
74 Gray Hairstreak: Strymon
melinus.
Purplish C.: Lycaena helloides.
American: L. americana.
Bronze: L. thoë.
75 Eastern-tailed: Everes
comyntas.
Marine: Leptotes marinus.
Spring: Lycaenopsis argiolus.
Western Pygmy: Brephidium
exilis.
76 Pieris rapae.
77 Common: Colias philodice.
Alfalfa: C. eurytheme.
78 Spicebush: Papilio troilus.
Parnassius: Parnassius
smintheus.
Giant: Papilio cresphontes.
79 Zebra: Papilio marcellus.
Black: P. asterius.
Tiger: P. glaucus.
81 Spicebush: Papilio troilus.
Zebra: P. marcellus.
Pipevine: P. philenor.
Black: P. asterius.
Giant: P. cresphontes.
Tiger: P. glaucus.
82 Arctic: Carterocephalus
palaemon.
Silver-spotted: Epargyreus
clarus.
Cloudy Wing: Thorybes
bathyllus.

83 Acrea: Estigmene acrea.
Banded Woollybear: Isia
isabella.
84 Protoparce quinquemaculata.
85 Celerio lineata.
86 Samia walkeri.
87 Hyalophora cecropia.
88 Callosamia promethea.
89 Antheraea polyphemus.
90 Automeris io.
91 Actias luna.
92 Ultronia: Catocala ultronia.
Clouded Locust: Euparthenos
nubilis.
93 Eacles imperialis.
94 Corn Earworm: Heliothis
umbrosus.
Eur. Borer: Pyrausta nubilalis.
95 Hemerocampa leucostigma.
96 Porthetria dispar.
97 Fall Webworm: Hyphantria
cunea.
Tent: Malacosoma sp.
98 Alsophila pometaria.
99 Sanninoidea exitiosa.
100 Carpocapsa pomonella.
101 Thyridopteryx
ephemeraeformis.
102 Anopheles: Anopheles sp.
Aedes: Aedes sp.
103 Culex sp.
104 Tipulidae.
105 Robber: Asilidae.
Deer: Chrysops sp.
March: Bibionidae.
Black Horse: Tabanus atratus.
106 Bluebottle: Calliphora sp.
Greenbottle: Phaenicia sp.
107 Syrphid: Syrphidae.
Tachinid: Tachinidae.
Bee: Bombylius major.
108 Drosophila melanogaster.
109 Six-spotted: Cicindela
sexguttata.
Purple: C. purpurea.
110 Macrodactylus subspinosus.
111 Popillia japonica.
112 Carrion: Silpha americana.
Black Carrion: S. ramosa.
113 Amer. Burying: Necrophorus
americanus.
Hairy Burying: N. tomentosus.
Hairy Rove: Creophilus
villosus.

114 Alaus oculatus.
115 Calasoma scrutator.
116 Lampyridae.
118 Nine-spotted: Coccinella
  novemnotata.
  Convergent: Hippodamia
  convergens.
119 Two-spotted: Adalia
  bipunctata.
  Fifteen-spotted: Anatis
  quindecimpunctata.
121 Epilachna varivestis.
122 Colo. Potato: Leptinotarsa
  decemlineata.
  Striped Blister: Epicauta
  vittata.
123 Twelve-spotted: Diabrotica
  undecimpunctata.
  Striped: Acalymma vittata.
125 Common: Crioceris asparagi.
  Spotted: C.
  duodecimpunctata.
126 Whirligig: Gyrinidae.
  Water Scavenger: Hydrophilus
  triangularis.
127 Dytiscus sp.
128 Phyllophaga sp.
129 Cotinus nitida.
130 Dung: Phanaeus vindex.
  Rhinoceros: Xyloryctes
  satyrus.
  Tumblebugs: Canthon laevis.
131 Unicorn: Dynastes tityus.
  Ox: Strategus antaneus.
132 Horn: Passalus cornutus.
  Stag: Pseudolucanus
  capreolus.
133 Darkling: Eleodes sp.
  Mealworm: Tenebrio molitor.
  Tile-horned: Prionus
  imbricornis.
134 Locust: Megacyllene robiniae.
  Elder: Desmocerus palliatus.
  Flat-headed: Buprestis rufipes.
  Pine Sawyer: Monochamus sp.
135 Cotton Boll: Anthonomus
  grandis.
  Plum: Conotrachelus
  nenuphar.
  Nut: Balaninus sp.
  Billbug: Sphenophorus sp.
136 Tremex columba.
137 Megarhyssa atrata.
138 Camponotus herculeanus.

139 Fire: Solenopsis geminata.
  Cornfield: Lasius niger.
140 Little Black: Monomorium
  minimum.
  Pharaoh's: M. pharaonis.
  Argentine: Iridomyrmex
  humilis.
141 Oak Apple: Amphibolips sp.
  Elliptical Goldenrod: Gnori-
  moshema gallaesolidaginis.
  Goldenrod: Eurosta
  solidaginis.
  Blackberry: Diastrophus sp.
142 Potter-: Eumenes fraternus.
  Mason: Ancistrocerus
  birenemaculatus.
143 Mud Dauber: Sceliphron
  caementarium.
  Cuckoo: Chrysis sp.
  Blue Mud: Chalybion
  californicum.
144 Velvet Ant: Dasymutilla sp.
  Cow Killer: D. occidentalis.
  Solitary Wasp: Ammophila
  aureonotata.
145 Sphecius speciosus.
146 Polistes annularis.
147 Bald-faced: Vespula maculata.
  Yellow Jacket: V. sp.
148 Bumblebee: Bombus sp.
  Sweat Bee: Halictus sp.
149 Leaf-cutting: Megachile sp.
  Honeybee: Apis mellifera.
  Flower: Augochlora sp.
150 Carpet: Anthrenus
  scrophulariae.
  Black Carpet: Attagenus
  piceus.
  Clothes: Tinea pellionella.
151 Dog Flea: Ctenocephalides
  canis.
  Sheep Tick: Melophagus
  ovinus.
  Duck Louse: Lipeurus
  squalidus.
153 Silverfish: Lepisma
  saccharina.
  Amer. Dog Tick: Dermacentor
  variabilis.
  Bedbug: Cimex lectularis.
  Larder: Dermestes lardarius.
  House Fly: Musca domestica.
  Ger. Cockroach: Blatella
  germanica.

INDEX

Asterisks (*) denote pages on which illustrations appear.

INDEX (continued)